Before He Finds YOU

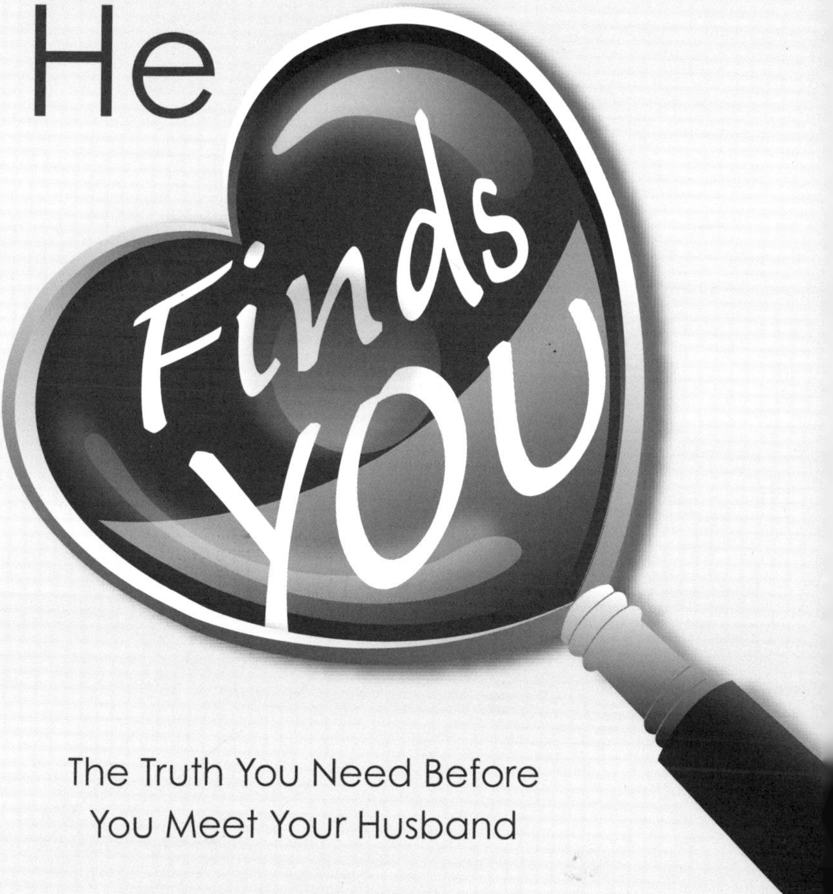

The Truth You Need Before You Meet Your Husband

Ebony Wright

Before He Finds You
Published by Marriage PLANS
13337 South Street, Suite 136
Cerritos, California 90703

ISBN 978-0-615-28515-3

Cover Design & Inside Layout: Connie Boone, Principal of *Creative Oxygen, Inc.*
Editor: Flo Jenkins, President of *Words That Flo!...An Editorial Consultancy Service,* located in Torrance, CA

Printed in China
2009 – First Edition

This book is dedicated to

My wonderful husband who is a walking, breathing manifestation of my prayers

My children who challenge me to grow and encourage me to keep doing the will of God

My parents who taught me well in the way of life

My Lord God who is my wisdom, my peace, my joy and the reason I exist

Contents

Testimonials

"I learned so many things about how we as women—and especially women of God—need to trust in God and look to Him in the process of selecting a husband."

~Maxine Stevenson, Divorced single-mother of two

"This book invites you to venture into a deeper intimacy with our Lord before you try to venture into a relationship with a potential husband. It opens your eyes to areas in your own life that you may not have been willing to give over to God because of past hurts or pain. In a very practical way, you are assisted in a journey into the 'deep unknowns' of your heart. Then, in His most gracious and loving way, God welcomes you into a place to hope and dream about your future once again, as His beloved daughter."

~ Mary Grace Cachuela, Founder and President,
InJOY Life Resources, Inc.

"I went through this book as a married woman thinking, 'There's nothing for me here. I already got my man!' As I dove into each chapter, I realized just how much I was out of alignment! This book challenged me to understand who I am in Christ, and who I am as a woman and a wife. It wasn't easy to swallow, but it was definitely worth it. I don't think this book is only for women who want to be married, but it is also for women who are already married. This is a must-read for any woman who wants to improve herself and her relationships!"

~ Stephanie Lainez, Author of *Rachel and the Lion*

"In working through this book I was able to look at my heart in an honest way. I was given an opportunity to let my heart be healed of past pain, while at the same time, my faith was stirred to believe God for the deep desires that He had already placed inside me.

Practically speaking, the material in this book led me to conversations with my two former boyfriends which set me free in ways I can't explain and wouldn't have expected. Following those conversations one of them got married, the other became engaged and I found myself in a new relationship—the first in four years—all within one week.

God has given Ebony an ability to speak the truth in love, without any compromise or sugarcoating. It's what every woman needs to hear. I'm so thankful for the gift this material has been to me, and the tangible transformation it has produced in my life."

~ Meg Votta, Development Coordinator, Philippines orphanage & Program Supervisor, InJOY Life Resources, Inc.

"This book ministered to me deeply. As a woman wanting to be married, I discovered that I should not be looking for Mr. Right, but instead be looking for more ways to be

closer to God. I know I need to have a strong relationship with God, seeking Him for all my needs and it is then, when my focus is on Him, that Mr. Right will find me."

~Monique Alegria, Single-mother of one

"This series is refreshingly honest and packed with love. Ebony translates God's love and plan for His girls into practical wisdom for honoring God in life through our imperfections in an often disappointing world. As a single woman who has made plenty mistakes in dating, I was challenged, encouraged and comforted all at the same time by this series. It highlighted Biblical principles that has given me a more Godly perspective in an area women often take into our own hands, relationships. Marriage PLANS invites readers to discover God's perfect plan for marriage and to enjoy the adventure."

~Natalie Allen, Thirty-something Single

"Single women are always looking for someone who can relate to them and understand their struggles. Ebony does an amazing job of sharing her story with humor and transparency of being a single woman discovering how to prepare for her future husband. It's encouraging to read that even if we've made some bad decisions in our lives that God is sovereign and He still has an incredible marriage waiting for us. This book isn't a secret formula on how to find your man but it is so much more! You will walk away challenged and liberated as you learn how to become the woman 'he' wants to find. I strongly believe every woman, single or married, should read this book to invest in themselves and in their relationships."

~Lizette Lujan, Women's Ministries Leader

"Everyone wants the 'how-to' for life and relationships. Everyone wants that manual for getting over a past love and for making your relationship with God #1. Every woman wants to know the how, when, what, where and—especially—who. Ebony's book is a brilliantly anointed lesson on the practical steps I need to take to become the woman/wife I need to be, and how to find peace as I wait on the Lord."

~Misty Shawn, Children's Ministry Leader

"This book is FANTASTIC! So down-to-earth, practical 'applied-wisdom' for ladies who desire to become wives of integrity or as I might coin it, 'covenant makers' who desire to present to their husband those things which are true, noble, just, pure, lovely, of good report, virtuous, and praiseworthy (Phil. 4:8). A woman 'after God's own heart.'"

~ Phil Waugh, Executive Director, Covenant Marriage Movement, Inc.

Preface

The Biggest Misconception

Thanks to popular culture, marriage is increasingly getting a bad rap, and in some states in America, it's being redefined altogether[1]. Sadly, despite the millions of men and women who *are* happily married, the worst of the worst seems to cloud the true blessing God designed marriage to be. Unfortunately, marriage has become an act of self-fulfillment that can easily be discarded, instead of the true covenant commitment of its original intent.

It's amazing that when God first created Earth and everything in it, the last thing He created on the sixth day was husband and wife. At that point, He declared that all He had created was good and then rested on the seventh day. He was done! For God, Adam and Eve were icing on the cake; a perfect union that complemented each other, and so important that He declared in Matthew 19:6, "let no man put [it] asunder." Marriage *is* good —better than good— when you first understand its true intent.

Before He Finds You is written for any woman, young or mature in age, who desires to be married—someday. It is especially designed to be most effective when read before a potential mate presents himself. Why? Because the best time to learn and study to be a wife is before you enter into a relationship. Similar to becoming a doctor, you don't start practicing medicine without any intense study and hope that you'll get better along the way. People's lives are at stake. It's literally a matter of life or death. Entering into marriage should be no different. The amount of preparation you put into becoming a wife is a direct correlation to the quality of life you will get out of your marriage. There will be plenty of hands-on

---

[1]Goodridge v. Dept. of Public Health, 11/18/03, Supreme Judicial Court of Massachusetts ruling on gay marriage.

learning after the wedding, but to build a strong foundation—without distraction—the learning starts now.

The goals of this book are:

1. To revive the desire in women to get married by dispelling pop culture myths.

2. To empower women to make wise and Godly decisions that will ultimately set them up for the most rewarding marriage possible.

3. To decrease the divorce rate by providing them the necessary tools to prevent some of the frustrating issues that lead to major problems.

And since nothing (tangible or intangible) exists inside of a vacuum, the byproducts of reaching these goals are widespread. For example, the negative impact of broken homes and marriages reaches beyond the obvious social implications and even affects our environment. Where resources were once shared in a nuclear home, resources are now doubly consumed (heating two homes instead of just one), trash increases (two empty bottles of dish soap instead of one) and space decreases (more homes with fewer occupants[2]). If more people get married and stay married, in a sense, they are automatically improving the health of our environment. Healthy marriages are vitally essential in the overall well being of our society and communities abroad. The principles taught here are intended to have results of epidemic proportions, setting up future generations for fulfilling, profitable marriages.

---

[2]Proceedings of the National Academy of Sciences, 12/18/07, vol. 104, no. 51

This process is designed to first, give you the information you need, then secondly, take you through a series of action steps to effect positive change in your life. The only way this works is if you ACTUALLY DO THE WORK. Completing each action step, one-by-one, in order, will help you build a foundation for your marriage that will not be easily shaken. Simply reading this book without engaging in the necessary actions will be useless to you. So, if you are not ready to do the work yet, I would recommend you save this book until you are serious about preparing yourself for marriage. Your training in integrity starts here, right now.

As you begin to go through each chapter and submerge yourself in the action steps, you'll begin to see three repeating themes:

1. Building a strong support circle of quality sisters and girlfriends.
2. Relying upon direction from God.
3. Focusing your energy on edifying yourself.

These three components, when used together, will yield you the greatest results in this preparation process, and beyond that, set you up for experiencing life at its most fulfilling capacity. The focus of this material is on marriage preparation, but the principles are universal and applicable to so many different areas of your life. This book will challenge you to focus on *all* of you—your whole person—because getting married is not an isolated event, but an all-encompassing life event, and all of you needs to be ready before you say, “I do.”

Enjoy this time of getting to know you and investing in yourself. It may very well be one of the most rewarding activities of your life.

Chapter 1

The One Worthy of Your Affections

All love begins with God.

Imagine him for a moment … the way he looks at you after a long day of anticipating your arrival. The way he holds you and all seems right with the world. How he always manages to bring a smile to your face. Think of how invincible you feel with him at your side. You truly believe you can be anything and do anything as long as he's right there cheering you on. How you admire him and adore him. How he always seems to have your best interest in mind. And how is it that he always knows exactly what you need before you can even figure it out yourself? Just to hear his voice … nothing is more soothing. You wake in the morning, filled with excitement as you anticipate your first contact with him for the day. Nobody—and I mean, NOBODY—loves you the way he does. Everything about you, he absolutely loves, unconditionally. Wow! If all that wasn't enough, it's amazing how he asks for so little in return.

You may be thinking, "Who is 'he' and where can I find one just like him?" Or maybe you already have someone in mind. The truth is, no matter what you were thinking, there's only one of Him, and fortunately for all of us, His heart is infinite and His affections toward us are endless. Don't know Him? His name is God, known affectionately through Jesus Christ. In Him is where *all* love begins.

He IS love[3]. In all of our efforts to conceptualize His greatness, it is impossible for any of us to fully understand how deep and wide His love for us really is. Even now, I fall short of just giving you an idea of God's vast love, since it is truly indescribable. In the purest sense, of all the things we think He wants from us, what He wants most is for us to love Him with all our hearts, all our souls and all our minds[4].

Until you know Him, your quest to find true love will be a series of trial and error type events that will begin to deplete your optimism over time. It is very difficult to identify something if you don't already know what it looks like. Contrary to what people may say, love is not subject to the interpretation of individuals. We don't have to guess or wonder, "Is this love?" There is a standard. If it doesn't bare any resemblance to God's love for us, then we can rest assured that an upgrade is on its way.

Love At First Encounter

Really, God just wants to be loved, adored and admired. He wants your affections, quality time with you and your thoughts. He wants your heart. And I know it may sound strange, but He is such a romantic. He knows better than you what makes your heart melt and how to make you feel loved. Who, but God, could see me staring hopelessly out the window, depleted of joy and send a hummingbird right up to my window to hover for a few moments before flying away? It instantly brought a smile to my face, because I knew God was saying, "I see you and you're going to be fine, Ebony. Cheer up." You can keep your stinkin' roses. God sends me hummingbirds.

He is never pushy or controlling, but with your permission He has the power to make your life far better than you could have ever dreamed[5]. He loves us tenderly and corrects us with love[6]. This is where you start if you ever really want to know what real love looks like. The "he" I was talking about in the beginning is Who God is, if

---

[3]I John 4:8, 4:16 | [4]Matthew 22:37-38 | [5]Ephesians 3:20 | [6]Proverbs 3:12

you invite Him in. Once you turn your affections toward Him, He will sweep you off your feet. Suddenly, you'll begin to notice all the times He sends you a little "pick me up" and be ever so grateful that there's finally someone who knows just how to make you feel priceless.

Honestly speaking, it may not be "love at first sight" for you toward a loving Father God. We are all humans experiencing this thing called life. Unfortunately, not everyone has a background that allows her (or him) to just open up and love freely—especially a God whom they cannot see. If you have been hurt in past relationships with men, a father, or a stranger for that matter, you may feel some resistance against throwing it all into the wind and putting yourself out there with vulnerability exposed on all sides. Whether it's betrayal, abuse, abandonment, or a violent act, they all can create a self-defense state of mind that says, "As long as I don't get too close to anyone, I won't get hurt like that again." And that may work for a while, but anything you resist, persists. If you continue to protect yourself from being hurt, you hurt yourself by preventing yourself from being *loved*. The most assuring trait of God for me is that He is not a man that can lie[7]. What He says, He does. He won't get you all worked up and hopeful only to turn around and leave you[8]. He won't love you today, and find a new love tomorrow.

Perhaps your issues are not with past hurts, but all this intimacy with someone you can't feel, touch or see. For some, this concept will seem too abstract to wrap your mind around, and you may even become frustrated because you just don't get it. Don't worry. God knows your heart and He knows just how to reach you. Just like you'd expect the water to run if you turned on the faucet, keep your faith and expect that God will respond to you. He will strengthen you if you are patient and wait on Him[9].

True, as in all love stories, there will be ups and downs. Your love affair with God will not be just one romantic spell after

---

[7]Numbers 23:19 | [8]Deuteronomy 31:6, 8; Joshua 1:5
[9]Psalm 27:14; Isaiah 40:31, 57:10

another. Yes, there will be times when you'll just feel His love pouring out on you, but there will also be times of "perceived" distance and frustration—on your part, not His. You will have to work in this relationship just like any other to maintain it and keep it fresh. Relationships are living entities that grow and feed. Things are great when they're feeding and getting fat, but when they're growing, we feel the strain as we move out of our comfort zones and into areas unfamiliar. So, don't grow weary in doing what's right. There is always a great reward for diligence[10]. These challenges will test your commitment to the relationship and serve as a barometer of your heart.

> *There is no end to what God's willing to go through with you.*

The difference between going through challenging times with God and challenging times with a man is that 1) God already has His stuff together, so it's never us waiting on Him to get some "act right," but it's Him waiting on us. He is 100% committed to seeing us be the best we can possibly be; 2) No matter how long it takes you to get it together and press through to the next level, He'll wait for you—no matter what; and 3) There really is no end, no plateau, no threshold to what He's willing to go through with you. He loves you more than you can imagine and knows there is victory on the other side.

A Personal Encounter

There have been quite a few times in my life when God has shown up in ways only God could. I remember once just feeling hurt and rejected by one *not* worthy of my affections. I was lying on my bed one cool afternoon, and as the warm rays of the sun shone through the blinds onto my face, I stared out the window. I remember saying to God, "Why does this hurt so much?" And as I lay there, completely still and totally quiet, I felt as if He put His arms around me and held me

[10]Galatians 6:8-10

close, and I'll never forget what He said next. He told me, "You haven't lost *anything*. It's *him* who's losing." As He continued to encourage me, it wasn't long before I got up off that bed feeling like "the unworthy one" was the one to pity. After that encounter, you couldn't tell me that I wasn't priceless. And there's not a soul I know who can make me feel the way God does because no one knows me like He does, and the same is true for you.

I feel really silly saying this, but He's really amazing in other areas too. Well, of course He is. He's God, a wellspring of wisdom. I was a single-mom for 8 years before getting married. The first half of those years I lived with my parents, but the last half I was on my own. During that time, I received welfare for 5 years, completed a Bachelor's degree in business, worked just under full-time status and somehow managed to take care of my child, pay rent, and save enough money to buy a reliable used car. Right after graduation, I was laid off from my job, and was no longer on welfare. Despite the situation, I never asked my parents or my child's father for a single dime, yet I made it through. My parents helped with childcare, but I cannot begin to tell you all the different times I needed God to do something magnificent or show me something amazing. It was through those tough times that God was really able to show me His heart and His love for me.

Looking For Love

Here we are, longing to be loved and adored, looking every which way for *something* that feels real *and* right, searching high and low in the natural, and yet it is God who seeks these things from us first. How I wish I could tell you so that you could truly understand that if you just take a chance on God, that which you have been searching for, He gives freely, abundantly, and greater than you could ever imagine. The best part of what you long for comes only from the One Who loves you most[11].

[11] 1 John 4:7; Psalm 36:4-6

You can give up your search for love and just *look* up. He's there where He's always been, waiting for you with open arms, already loving you more than you know, and ready to take you as far as you're willing to go.

Building Intimacy

Be vulnerable and invite Him in. He already knows everything about you, but there's an amazing bond that takes place when you trust Him enough to open up and give Him your account in your own words. Make Him your first love, court Him and get to know Him. Sure, you can't call Him on the phone or make reservations for two or play a game of tic-tac-toe with Him, but you can call Him anytime, anywhere, enjoy dinner with Him, or take a stroll on the beach with Him. All it requires is that you set your focus on Him and open your heart and ears. He's never late and is always good company. If you let Him in, you'll find that none compare. He always forgives you, He thinks you look beautiful in the morning—without your makeup—and always knows just how to encourage you when you're up against the wall. And that's not even the tip of the iceberg. When you think about how He so carefully and intricately formed us, there's no denying His intense interest in us.

Be open to Him and just say what's on your heart. You don't have to get super religious and speak in Christian-ese. God speaks your language and knows your vernacular. All prayer is, is dialogue with God. Be real with Him, and above all, be honest. The strongest relationships are built on honesty and trust. When you're done talking, be still and allow Him to speak back to you. This may take some getting used to since God has been known to speak in "a gentle whisper[12]." It will often require you to shut down all distractions in your environment *and* in your mind. It will take some time before you are able to master it, but God is always talking, urging, and

---

[12] I Kings 19:12

directing. Most of us are just too busy to notice. Get used to hearing His voice. It will help you develop your discernment. Ignoring it could literally cost you your life. Not unlike your relationship with your future husband, the success of your relationship with God depends a great deal on good communication.

Before I met my husband, I took a six-month sabbatical from dating men and dated God instead[13]. We'd dine together, go to the movies, sit on the beach, go to the spa, or just sit on the couch and do nothing—just God and me. Of course, to everyone else, it may have looked as though I was lonely or didn't have any friends available to accompany me, but I had such a peace about the time I spent with God. Family or friends would have been an intrusion on my time with God and a distraction. It was my favorite time of the week and I protected it fiercely. A lot of the time He'd talk to me and show me things, while other times we were just comfortably silent. It was a time for me not only to get to know God on a more intimate level, but also for me to get to know myself and love myself more. Even now that I'm married, I still cherish my time out "alone" (even if it's just a run to the grocery store), because that's time I spend with God to get recharged and to reconnect with my first love.

I remember being out with God once, and while I was waiting in line to purchase a movie ticket, there was a small group of high school aged girls in front of me, one of which was very social. While they were talking and giggling, she turned around and saw that I was standing alone in line and asked, "Are you here by yourself?" When I said yes, she tilted her head, looked at me with pity in her eyes and said, "Oh, how sad." When I grinned and asked her why such was the case, she said something about not having anyone to talk to and being lonely. I told her, "I'm not lonely. I'm *with* myself and I actually really enjoy it. You should try it sometime." But, I could tell from the look on her face, she didn't get it. I just smiled as she turned back to

---

[13]Knight in Shining Armor, P.B. Wilson

her friends to tell them how sad it was that I was alone. It tickled me, but I remember hoping that one day she would understand. Maybe I was selfish to not share with her Whose company I was actually in. I just didn't want to spend my time with Him, talking to her. Now that I know Him a whole lot better, I don't mind sharing with others when we're out one-on-one. He's so "full of wonderful," there's always enough for everyone.

I encourage you to take a deliberate sabbatical from dating and just date God instead. I say "deliberate" because you will not get the same results if you say, "I'm already doing that. I haven't dated in several months." That is not the same as saying, "I am focusing my energy on being with God and being ever mindful that He is with me at all times." This may seem strange, but although God is Spirit, He is also a person. Treat Him as such. Sometimes when I am alone, driving down the street, I like to envision God sitting right next to me in the passenger seat and I may reach out to Him by putting my hand on the seat. This helps me be more conscious of Him and not forget that He's right there with me. So, when you go on your date with God, put on your makeup, fix your hair just right and even toil over which outfit to wear. The more real you make it, the greater your reward. Besides, who else deserves your best but God anyway?

Spend time with God every day.

Good Habits Start Now

Once God has opened your eyes and Mr. Wonderful shows up, you'll find that while he won't compare to God, you'll be acutely aware of his qualifying characteristics because you'll see in him traces of those same characteristics that make God so great. The reality is, even after you're married, you will still **need** God in many of the same ways you needed Him before. This is so because your husband, as wonderful as he'll be, **will** mess up, say the wrong things, and do the wrong things. He will, he will, he will! That's why it's so important to spend some time every day with God. You can never know Him enough. Pray, read His Word, listen to teachings, and really gain a strong presence of Him in your heart and mind.

Your relationship with God *will* change once you're married though[14]. Because you will have more distractions dividing your attention, you may feel like the honeymoon with God is over now. Don't be surprised if you find yourself longing for the relationship you had with God when you were single. You will have to make adjustments and grow to a new level with God just like you would in any other relationship when change occurs. This is the primary reason it's so beneficial to develop a strong relationship with Him now. It will be more of a sacrifice and more challenging to try to really develop it later when the heat is on. Good habits now will go a long way. It will help secure your foundation and be a rock to you in challenging times. And when you're going through it because your husband just doesn't understand you, you'll find it comforting to know that you can turn to Someone Who does—Someone Who still knows exactly what to say.

No Thanks

Undoubtedly, there will be some reading this who will say, "This God and Jesus stuff is just not for me" or "I don't really think it requires all that." I realize there will be critics and skeptics who will wonder what place this really has in a book about marriage. Many will believe they can bypass this portion and just be a good person with good intentions. To them I say, "To each his own."

Will this book benefit those of a different faith or belief system? Probably. Can I vouch for the quality or success they may or may not have? No. I can only share what I know works and what I

[14]I Corinthians 7:34

know is the Word of God. Some of what I share are basic principles and laws that God set up in the earth. Since they're laws, they will work if you practice them—whether you confess Jesus as Lord and Savior or not (i.e. what you reap is what you sow). But for the most part, a great deal of your success in this process will rely upon you: 1) trusting God, 2) hearing from God and 3) obeying what you've heard from God. Without these three crucial elements, this book is just a book of rules that can be broken when you see fit, with no consequence. Taking God out of the equation or downplaying the role God has in this process will diminish the favor, grace, and mercy you will need to make the best decisions possible. Everything you learn from this point forward will build and depend on Who you believe God is and what you believe He's capable of doing.

So, before you go any further, ask yourself, "Who is *He* to me?"

Action for Chapter 1

"Delight yourself in the LORD and he will give you the desires of your heart." –Psalm 37:4

The objective of the first action step is to create or intensify your relationship with God. If you have not yet formally received Christ into your heart, please see Appendix 1 for "How to Enter into a Relationship with Christ" before attempting the following action steps.

The following steps will help you create a strong foundation for a relationship with God.

Reduce distractions: TV, radio, phone, email, and anywhere else you may be overextending yourself.

Take 6 – 12 months off from dating so that you can get to know God intimately.

Tend to your relationship with God.

a. If you are building a relationship with God for the first time:

- **i.** Start by spending just 5 minutes each morning with God. At first it will seem like a lifetime, but as you get to know Him better, the time will fly by.
- **ii.** Spend two minutes in thanksgiving, a minute or two just talking to God, and the remainder of time in silence, just being still.
- **iii.** Consider adding worship music to your time. You can find great music in the Contemporary Christian or Gospel genres.
- **iv.** Begin journaling your time with God and any observations you find.
- **v.** Gradually increase your time, over time.
- **vi.** Commit to reading one chapter of the Bible a day.
- **vii.** Continue to build to the following level.

b. If you are rekindling or re-energizing your relationship with God:

- **i.** Spend 30 minutes to an hour with God each day. Be sure to reserve some time to just being still and listening.

ii. Begin keeping a prayer journal of what God is telling you, your requests to Him, and documenting when those prayers are answered.

iii. Spend more time listening to Christian music throughout your day (while working or driving, doing chores, etc.). Doing so builds up a storehouse of positive thoughts and phrases that will get into your subconscious and randomly remind you of God's promises.

iv. Make a date time for just you and God, once a week. Go out and do something together: dinner, movies, skating, beach, shopping, museums, etc.

v. Listen for how God would like to take your relationship to the next level.

If you don't already have one, find a good Bible-teaching church where you can plant yourself, flourish and develop encouraging relationships (Hebrews 10:24-25, Psalm 92:13).

Connect with another woman whom you feel has a great relationship with God and has some knowledge of God's Word. She will be your cheerleader and encourage you in your spiritual growth. She will also be there to answer any questions you may have on your journey.

You will continue to grow and develop your relationship from this point forward. The goal is to overwhelm the negative thought processes in you with God's Word. Once you have been consistent for at least two weeks, move on to the next chapter and begin to build on your foundation.

Chapter 2

"Pardon Me, Are You Single?"

So, there you are in the grocery store after a long day's work. Your mind is on getting in and out as quickly as possible so that you're not up late eating dinner at 10 o'clock again. You move swiftly down the pasta aisle, and as you're looking for your favorite ready-made sauce, you notice a gentleman a few feet away who also seems to be looking for something—or at least he *was* until you caught him stealing a glance at you. You quickly weigh the options and decide to stay on task so you can get your tired-self home. Just as you grab the sauce off the shelf and set it in your cart, Mr. Possibility approaches you with a smile and humbly asks, "Excuse me … but are you single?"

What do you say? Chances are, if you're reading this book and you are not currently committed to someone, you'd say, "… Yes." But, I want to challenge you in that response and ask you, "Are you, really?"

Maybe, technically, there's no man currently in your life. But have you really gotten over the one whom you invested so much of your heart into, but somehow things just didn't work out? Have you forgiven the one who took your heart for everything it was worth and then left you with nothing? Have you let go of the possibility that maybe one day, the one you secretly long for will suddenly wake up and realize you are the love of his life? Or how about the friend—who's just a friend—but emotionally speaking, no one could take his place? And do I even have to mention the one you're not really committed to, but the two of you have this "understanding" that whenever one is in need of some sexual healing, the other is available? And just because I didn't specifically mention your special situation, that doesn't mean you're off the hook. The mere fact that *you* thought of it, qualifies it as one to consider.

Being single is more than being able to say you're not seeing anyone. Being single is just that, *single*: a state of oneness. Not you and whatever man you are holding onto in your heart. It doesn't matter if you are physically together or not. What matters is whether or not you are bound to him emotionally. Every time you hold on to a man that you are not mutually committed to, he occupies a space in your heart. After two or three men, do you really have room for another? Can you really give Mr. Possibility your all if there are three other men using up your energy? Even if you think so, is it really fair?

Unreciprocated commitment occupies space in your heart.

Soul Ties

There's this phenomenal thing that occurs when two people engage in sexual intimacy. Instantly a bond is created that tethers the two together and draws the two together in a way that is truly indescribable. It's a bond that is not easily broken so that if there is ever any adversity in the relationship, it will encourage the bond to continue for as long as possible. This is God's design for husbands and wives, which is why **not** engaging in premarital sex is important for more reasons than just disease and pregnancy. The two souls become united, hence, "and the two will become one flesh; so that they are no longer two but one."[15] God said it Himself. This is one of the reasons why divorce and some breakups are so devastating and painful; there is a near literal

[15] Mark 10:8

ripping of the flesh that happens when that "one" becomes two parts again. And often after the separation, it may take months—or even years—before those involved ever feel whole again. When it comes to sex, there are multiple layers to address, and we'll do more of that in chapter 7 and in Books 2, 3, and 4 of this series.

So, what if you've never been *sexually* involved with the man you considered three paragraphs ago? Here is where we find one of the ways God has made us genuinely feminine. As women, we have a unique piece to us that is not typically prominent in men. It is the part that helps us to express ourselves with tears, whether happy or sad. It's what moves us to care for and nurture others. It drives our passions and ignites our rage. It has an infamous reputation that popularized the saying, "a woman scorned …" and at the same time benefits the world with "… a woman's touch" or "a mother's love." It refers to how we could literally put our heart and soul into something and expect the best. I'm talking about our emotions. And when they are in action, they are a force to be reckoned with.

This is why emotional ties are nearly as significant for women as physical ones. Anything we pour our heart and soul into, we don't give up easily, even when we *know* it's not good for us. Letting go is distressing, and since we get our fair share of pain by default of being an emotional woman, anytime we can avoid it or trade it for another pain less intense, we do so without thinking about the long-term effects. Think about all the garbage we pack around with us: past hurts from friends and family, disappointments, and frustrations. Deep down, we know we'd be better off if we just dealt with these issues and moved on, but I think most of us will admit that it's easier to just tuck it in our internal trunk of junk.

Taking time to intensely examine your emotional investments and the relationships you currently have with the men in your life will help you begin the purging process. I'm not saying you shouldn't have male friends—in fact, you should. Men provide an outlook on life that is impossible for women to perceive on their own. They help simplify situations we sometimes overcomplicate. They can provide valuable insight in a variety of areas of your life and provide expertise in areas you have no interest in developing (like what kind of oil you should ask for when you get the oil changed in your car). However, examine just how much you depend on your guy friend emotionally. How much does *he* depend on *you*? Do you tell him *everything*? Is he your place of safety? Are you so close, others question how platonic you really are? Are you more affectionate with him than you would be with your brother? Are you emotionally intimate? Do you feel any obligation toward him? If you find yourself in one or more of these situations, it would be a good idea to scale back a bit so that you are able to respond to him more objectively. The last thing you want to happen when Mr. Wonderful shows up is to have your attention and loyalties divided. You may get Mr. Wonderful to be "understanding" of your "friend" in the beginning, but don't expect that to last once he gets a real sense of just how important your friend is to you. Because we are creatures of habit, in time of need, you will instinctively still turn to your guy friend first, because you know what he can offer and he feels safe. This will turn Mr. Wonderful on his heels faster than you can say, "But I can explain."

For all of my adolescent years and well into adulthood, my closest friend was a guy. While we didn't spend a great deal of time together or talk very often on the phone, we stayed in contact often enough to have a good idea of what was going on in each other's lives at any given point. Of all my friends, I found him to be the most trustworthy because he was simple and frank. Things were black and white for him, without all the differing shades of grey that we, as women, tend to focus on. And since I had a similar frankness, we got along very well, never being offended by one another. If I needed to vent or get an honest opinion, I felt safe calling on him because he was consistent. I grew up with younger brothers, but this friend was the big brother I never had, and he treated me much like the younger sister he never had.

It literally wasn't until the day I got the wedding invitation in the mail that I realized some day, our friendship would end as I knew it. It had never crossed my mind that one day, one of us would get married and the conversations that we had with one another would be replaced by conversations with our own spouses. Furthermore, I thank God for allowing me to see that for years I had been defaulting to this friend instead of God for wisdom and direction. It was in this time that my relationship with God really began to flourish and grow into something indescribably awesome. Over time, God realigned our friendship to its proper position, and along with our spouses, we are able to keep in touch and break bread together every couple of years or so.

Clean House

Ask God to help purge your spirit of all the men with whom you have become one, either physically or emotionally. It isn't necessary to broadcast or hold a conference call with these men to tell them what you're doing. This will often prompt them to discourage you from doing what you know you should, and strategize to keep you deeply involved. At this point in the process, you just aren't strong enough to stand against it alone. Practically speaking, at the next urge to turn to this guy in emotional distress, turn to God instead, and put accountability partners in place (women friends you trust) whom you can call when you're feeling weak. The more open you are with your feelings and intentions, the faster the process will go. Denial and secrets incubate pain and shame. If you can't talk about it, you can't be delivered from it, so talk it up. Your women friends will be there for you when the longings are at their worst, and then turn you over to God to see you through. Set firm boundaries with those being purged, whether it be not taking their calls, eliminating your phone calls to them, and/or blocking or ignoring their texts, instant messages and emails. What's most important is that you stick to those boundaries with fierceness until the slightest temptation is over. This process is deeper than avoidance or "out of sight, out of mind." You'll need to avoid prolonged periods of daydreaming of him, and have an emergency plan to combat those thoughts. Don't be fooled. Purging will **not** be easy and don't be surprised if you feel like you are at war, emotionally.

Purging is deeper than avoidance; it's combatting your thoughts.

Personally speaking, while I was able to make a clean break from most of my past, one relationship, in particular, really challenged me in my commitment to the purging process. Maybe it was because he had been a permanent fixture in my life for nine years, or perhaps I could credit it to the three times we had been intimate over those nine years; or maybe it was because I had sold myself the idea that there couldn't be a better match for me. Whatever it was, those last three years he was in my life, I vacillated between "I gotta purge him" and "I gotta have him" so many times, he once told me that I was crazy. And I was. I heard God VERY clearly when He said, "You can't be with him," but I tried to negotiate with God and stretch it out as long as I could. Because of that, I have a personal revelation of what it means to be a double-minded person, unstable in all their ways.[16] I eventually insisted on my own way and God let me have it so that I could see for myself what He was trying to save me from. Less than six months later, I suddenly (after what seemed like a minor infraction) had a light bulb go on in my head, and I was able to break free from the tie that

---

[16] James 1:8

had gripped me for years. Did it have to take me three years? Of course not. I chose the hard path when I chose not to obey God immediately. But now I share my story so that you don't have to make the same mistakes I did. If God says no, He means no and for *good* reason.

Once you've been in the trenches for a while, you can gauge your progress by asking, "How would I handle it if I were to see him today?" If you aren't sure, you aren't done. When you begin to feel a peace about where you stand, you can make an intelligent decision about which male friends you can keep as strictly platonic **and** guarded, and which ones just aren't healthy for you. How long your purge takes is completely unique to your individuality. Maybe it will take one month, maybe three years. It really depends on how disciplined you are and how serious you are about freeing yourself up. In order to truly be single, you'll have to 1) be committed to the purging process, and 2) actually take action. Nothing changes by simply wishing it would.

"By the way, were you looking at me?"

Now that you know you are definitely single, you are able to answer Mr. Possibility in the grocery store with a confident, "Yes." After you exchange pleasantries, he suddenly asks you, "Excuse me for asking. I couldn't help but notice; were you looking at me? It seemed like you were trying to get my attention ..." Now, you and I both know he was mistaken because you almost walked away without so much as a smile. Then he goes on, " ... You know, last Friday?" Suddenly, you realize you've seen him before. Oh my goodness! This is the same guy you saw with his friends in the restaurant last Friday night while you were out with your best girlfriend. Only then, you weren't so unconcerned. Constantly primping your hair and clothes, multiple trips to the restroom so he'd have an opportunity to stop you, laughing louder than necessary in case he forgot you were still sitting there, and staring at him, then sheepishly turning away every time he felt your high beams glaring in his direction. Not so subtle, is it? Now, you're thoroughly embarrassed as he innocently recalls you from the restaurant. Or maybe you think, "Yes! Now it's my opportunity to make my full on impression." Let me forewarn you, don't be disappointed if he doesn't pursue you any further or if he does, you find out he's just looking for a little fun.

If you've never heard this Proverb, now is as good a time as ever to get a good understanding of it, "He who finds a wife, finds a good thing and obtains favor from the Lord"[17]. Let's break this down into three parts.

1. "He who finds a wife..."

He finds you. It may seem that I'm stating the obvious, but it's amazing how much energy some women put into actively looking for the right man. If a certain "he" doesn't find you on his own, it becomes evident that he is either not looking or he's not looking *for you*. For example, let's look at your potential husband in a slightly different scenario.

Say someone walked up to him—out of the blue—and handed him a key (this key represents who you are to him). Technically, he can't say he found that key, because he wasn't looking for it. And he wasn't looking for it because he either didn't need it or he didn't want it. Now, out of curiosity, he may hold on to that key for awhile in case he finds out what it's for, but until he does (and chances are pretty high that he won't), that key just sits in some junk drawer for an undetermined amount of time. On the other hand, let's say his great-grandfather leaves him his collection of antique sports cars that are

[17]Proverbs 18:22

locked away in a garage. When he tries to access the garage, he realizes he isn't in possession of the key. I'm willing to bet he'd search high and low until he found **this** key because now it's perceived value to him is priceless. Any ol' key someone hands him just won't do, so he immediately loses interest in the key in the junk drawer. He has to find that one key that gives him access to his fortune. How rewarding is it for him when he finally finds the key and now holds in his hand the rights to a priceless treasure?

You don't want to put yourself in a position where you become the junk drawer key and are suddenly sideswiped by the garage key. This does not mean you walk around blind to the world until some man apprehends you. Live your life to the fullest. Don't get passive and stop going after your heart's desires. Go for it! Buy that house, travel the world, start that business that's been brewing in your heart for years. God does not give you passions to hold on to, but to live out[18]. God has placed your husband in your world, but he won't find you if you aren't living there yet. Continue to do the things you love, and master the art of not pursuing while being acutely alert.

"But what if he needs help?" you ask. He doesn't. Men are like bloodhounds when it comes to finding a suitable wife. They know exactly what they want and don't need any help from you throwing distractions in their path. Also, men find purpose in problem solving. If you try to offer yourself as the "solution" to his "problem" of being wifeless, he is likely to be unreceptive since he didn't come to that conclusion on his own. Besides, if he needs help finding a wife, how many other countless things in life will he be dependent upon you for?

---

[18]Proverbs 13:12

2. "...finds a good thing..."

As his wife, he will find immeasurable value in you. To him, you are his missing rib. A long lost part of him that he's missed all his life until now. That's why when he meets you, maybe even before he knows you're his wife, he's drawn to you. You make him want to be a better man and he strives to become so. You are his "good thing" and everyone around him knows it. He's a different person since you've come into his life. You are able to tap into his unrevealed potential. As a result, *you* become more charged, and the intensity of your own potential increases. If he doesn't become a better man than he was before he met you, you are still a "good thing," just probably not his.

3. "...and obtains favor from the Lord."

Quite simply, once a man finds his good thing, the Lord blesses him with favor. He is rewarded for uniting with his helpmeet, enabling God a higher return on His investment of creating that man in the first place. When the two of you unite, spiritually, you are exponentially stronger than you are apart. God is all about increase. The husband and wife partnership means that together, they can now do more as a team for the sake of the Kingdom. Wherever two or three are gathered in Jesus' name, He is there in the midst of them[19]. And if the husband gets favor, by default of the

His reward for finding you is God's favor.

[19]Matthew 18:22

union, the wife gets some, too. That being said, don't get ahead of yourself and mess up your own favor by trying to find your own husband. There is a domino effect of blessings that occur when you allow yourself to be found. Your only job is to be alert and be ready. And of course, it doesn't hurt to be friendly and noncritical. Your future husband is most attracted to you when you are immersed in the fullness of you—the good and the bad. Being sincere and not pretending to be someone you aren't are sure to catch his attention. So, only spend time on the driving range if you really love golf. Don't go there with the intentions of snagging a potential mate or you'll end up frustrated with how much time he spends there once you're together, and he'll be left wondering why you don't understand. Just be you. The faster you get ready, the easier it will be for him to recognize you.

One More Thing

Just in case you still don't understand, "naming and claiming" your husband goes against the natural order of God. You can "name and claim" the promises of God, but you cannot pray your will over another human being. This is sure to bring confusion into any relationship that follows. Feelings of guilt and doubt are sure to arise as one or both of you begin to wonder if this is what he really wanted. The bottom line is that we want our future husbands to want us with a longing only second to God. Remember, God knows what you need better than you do, but if you insist upon what you want, He won't stop you. God won't force you to do anything. Just don't be mad at God when things don't go as you planned. I can assure you, God saw trouble coming long before you even got your hopes up.

If you believe that God has told you who your husband is, but you have no idea if God was polite enough to let that man know (as if that was possible), it's best to stay open until you get confirmation. And your only confirmation would be a proposal. Otherwise, you will build your hopes and dreams around someone who's essentially missed it. Then when God calls another man in to step up to the position, not only will you not receive it, you won't even recognize it. Just like you wouldn't buy a house that you aren't sure you'd ever be able to move into, you don't commit to a husband without knowing that he's heard clearly from God **and** is prepared to act on it. Otherwise, you could find yourself waiting for years to "move in" or fighting with the "previous occupants." When you think of this in terms of a husband, it's hardly ideal.

Freeing yourself up and trusting in God's way will make this stage in the process far less painful than if you had grown impatient and tried to work it out yourself.

Action for Chapter 2

"Perseverance must finish its work so that you may be mature and complete, not lacking anything." – *James 1:4*

Here are some steps to guide you through your journey to singleness:

Make a list of the men you need to purge.

- Don't cut corners. You'll have to be ruthless in this step to get true results.

Enlist support.

- Find two or three women who will be available to you to coach you through the tough times. CHOOSE THESE WOMEN WISELY. You will not be able to do this alone.

Pray and fast.

- Do this until you are released from those whom you are bound to. For more information on how to fast or fasting, take a fieldtrip to any Christian bookstore. I personally recommend *Fasting* by Jentezen Franklin.

Read the book of Esther in the Bible.

- This amazing story of Esther provides a perfect balance of forwardness, humbleness, preparedness, and being in the right place at the right time.

Chapter 3

Will You Know It When You See It?

I have a 9-year old son who LOVES to see and learn about new things. His curiosity and excitement is so pure and concentrated, it can actually move me to be interested in something I would never look at twice. Sometimes I look at him and think, "Wow, to be a kid again and see so many things with fresh and eager eyes must really make life worth living." On the other hand, focused trips to the toy store can be quite frustrating and time consuming. *Everything* catches his eye, while he picks up one item after another—each with its own declaration of amazement, "Ooo, Mom, look at this! I didn't know they have that! That over there is cool! Wow! I always wanted one of these!" This hyper-charged rant of activity will go on indefinitely unless I give him some very defined parameters in which to focus his attention. At first, I used to let him go on and on, then try to get him to focus once our time began to run short. This was only partially effective because now that he had seen *sooo* many things, he couldn't remember what he really liked and had a difficult time making a final selection. Now, before we even leave the house, he is required to have in mind what it is he really wants. He can still look around a bit, but he already knows what he's looking for, so making the final selection is a far simpler process.

Being able to identify the right man when he comes along can be a lot like my son going into a toy store with no focus in mind. Everything looks cool to my son at first, but after a minute or two, he quickly moves on to something seemingly more interesting until he can't commit to anything for fear he'd choose the wrong thing. This is what we call "dating." Trying out this guy for a while and when he doesn't work out, you try out another and another until you find the right one. Problem is, we usually tire out before that happens, because a string of unsuccessful encounters leads us to believe there are not any good men left. You can eliminate some of the frustration simply by getting focused *before* you put yourself out on the scene.

Think about it: Everything you've ever wanted in your life, you've either seen with your eye or with your mind's eye. Even if you can't describe the mechanics, you still have an image or idea of some sort to connect with that desire. Anything ever created was first seen in the mind of the creator. The more vivid the vision, the easier it is to create. So what's all this about?

You have to first have a vision of the kind of man God would have you to marry before you can identify if a man is worthy, otherwise, anything will do as long as he's "nice enough" or a "good person" (as far as you can tell). In recent times, there has been a growing popularity in what many call "the list." In case you aren't familiar, "the list" is basically a wish list of what you want in a husband. Some praise it, while others have literally cast theirs into a burning fireplace. I, personally, am a supporter of "the list" for obvious reasons: I had one and it worked beautifully. My husband is a living, breathing, walking manifestation of my list. Was I lucky? Not at all. I always say, "Who needs luck when you have Jesus?" The difference between the list that works and the one that doesn't is rooted in perspective.

> *The difference between a list that works and one that doesn't, is perspective.*

Perspectives

The *easy* way to create your list is through your own perspectives; drawing on past experiences, things you've observed in movies and in others' relationships, and pure imagination. Using this perspective, your list will grow and grow and grow because there really is no end to the number of ways your prince could be charming. After all, your dream man is perfect. Unfortunately, there is no such thing as a perfect man—on planet Earth anyway. So while you are holding fast to this dreamy vision, Girl, you might as well pin a boutonnière on it and take it to the courthouse, because the only place your man exists is on paper. Besides, the only person worthy of a perfect man is a perfect woman. And although we think we have it all together, you and God (and everyone else who loves you) know that simply isn't true. No matter how much you think God will give you the desires of your heart and make your list a reality, you will be disappointed on this one. God only created one perfect man and He is seated at the right hand of God. But don't fret. There is still a way for you to see God give you everything you need, plus more than you ever wanted … change your perspective[20].

Forget about your past experiences and what *you* think you need, and ask God to give you a fresh perspective of the qualities and characteristics of the man He has for you. I promise you, this list will be very different from the one created using the above perspective. This list does not include physical characteristics like height, weight and skin color. It won't dictate what kind of investments he has, how much money he makes a year or what kind of car he drives. It doesn't take into consideration where he lives, where he's from or where he works. He will not have to live up (or down) to your educational requirements or be a prominent figure in the community. He will simply have to have a heart that is open and submitted to God. God knows you better than you know yourself. He knows what personality and

---

[20]Psalm 37:4

temperament to pair together with you to yield the greatest return in exploits for Him, and love and fulfillment for you.

Often because of our humanness, we erroneously look for and consider the wrong things in our soul mate. In 1Samuel 16, God had sent Samuel to Bethlehem to crown a new king of Israel. As men approached, Samuel tried to guess who God had selected based on their stature and appearance. But God quickly corrected him and said in verse 7, "Do not consider his appearance or his height, for I have rejected him. The LORD does not look at the things man looks at. Man looks at the outward appearance, but the LORD looks at the heart." (NIV) This is the perspective we **must** use when creating "the list," or it will surely fail. Does that mean your man won't be appealing to you? Of course not! But chances are, he may not look anything like what you thought was "your type." There's only one Who knows what you like and need better than you do, and that's God.

While we look at outward appearances, God looks at the heart.

Getting Started

So how, exactly, do you find out what God's perspective is on this matter? First, God has tons of things to say in regards to what makes a good husband and wife, and how they can honor Him and have the most fulfilling life together. All this can be found in the Bible. You'll want to use a translation that's easy to read so that you fully understand what He is saying (e.g. NIV). At the end of this chapter, there is a partial list of scriptures that speak directly to the character of husbands and wives and what you should be looking for.

Secondly, in your private prayer time, allow God the opportunity to speak to you. Write down what you feel He is saying in your spirit, even if you never thought of it before. He will give you some things specific to your background, interests, and beliefs. After all, if your ideal family is a husband, wife and 4 children, He's not going to hook you up with someone who'd rather breed pit bulls than procreate.

Start to write the vision and make it plain[21]. As you begin to seek God, ask Him to show you what you need in a husband. Do this as soon as you can and *before* you meet a potential candidate. If you wait until after Mr. Big & Handsome walks into your life, you'll be faced with the daunting task of having to look into his dreamy eyes and make difficult decisions. You may be tempted to ignore certain things or make unwise exceptions, because once you've set your heart on something, your mind will begin to compensate for you to make that thing manifest.

Be honest with yourself and God on every point you put on your list. Carefully label several critical points with "MUST have." This could be a deal breaker in an otherwise promising candidate. For example, if you know one of your greatest desires in life is to be a mother, and he is fabulous in every way except he is not interested in being a father, then it would be a grave mistake to hook up with him and hope he changes his mind. You'll both end up miserable. It is better to let this guy go. He is perfect for some other woman, but not for you.

Likewise, there may be an item or two that you could probably live without, if necessary. Label these accordingly. Let's say, as an illustration, you really love to dance. Well, if your potential mate is not much of a dancer, do you throw out the baby with the bath water? Heavens, no! Just make sure he doesn't mind if you turn on the radio and get your groove on with your girlfriends every now and then.

Most importantly, don't modify your list based on what you see in your environment, what you've seen on others' lists, or at the

---

[21]Habakkuk 2:2

prompting of a friend or family member. Better yet, keep your list private. It is a prayer of agreement between you and God. The last thing you want to happen is to have some well-intentioned loved one distract you from what you KNOW came from God.

Be as thorough as possible, but know that inevitably, something will slip through the cracks. It will be something you never even thought of, or something that is so evident, it won't come to mind. Don't worry. This is God's doing. There are some things that we think we want or don't want, but God knows better. These will be the things that you'll say, "I never thought I would've wanted x-y-z, but now that I have it, it's been a real blessing, and I've grown and learned so much from it." God *is* genius. You couldn't dream up a better match for yourself if you tried.

My Story

When I wrote my "list," there were 29 items on it. Only one of them had to do with appearance, and that was that he was well groomed and had good hygiene. Looking at my list now, none of them have anything to do with money, but it was important that he had vision and ambitions. When you understand what marriage is for and the favor you are to this man when you marry, he doesn't need to have a whole lot going on financially, as long as he has a vision and a plan. Once you show up, you begin to spark things in him that have been simmering for a long time, and pretty soon you'll get an explosion. I'm not saying he couldn't do it without you, but just not with the same grace and favor. As women, we have the ability to release potential through influence. All you need to know now is if he has any to be released.

Once I had the list, I used it as a prayer guide and prayed these things over him daily. Doing this will greatly increase the success of your list because you are now speaking your list into existence, from your mouth to God's ear. Additionally, if you haven't already covered it on your list, pray for his health, welfare, career, mind, spiritual growth, patience, or whatever else comes up in your spirit. God knows who your husband is today, even if you don't. Just because you can't look him in the eye or tell someone what his name is, doesn't mean God doesn't know whom you're talking about when you say, "my husband." After all, He's omniscient and knows the end from the beginning[22]. If you want him to arrive to you in "ready position," start covering him now. Praying for your husband is a practice that will need to be carried on throughout your entire marriage, so why not start now? Furthermore, when you do finally meet, something in your spirit will be confirmed, because you will see your prayers standing live before your face. What better way to see God glorified[23]?

Your prayers help your future husband arrive in ready-position.

Be careful that you don't prematurely name your husband before he declares his intent. Postpone praying for him by name until after you are engaged. Instead, continue to pray for your unnamed husband. Additionally, pray over the one who's presented himself until his intentions become clear and public. Anytime you commit yourself to doing something God's way, there will immediately be tests and challenges. You don't want to start calling your husband by name if he has not shown you that he is ready to commit by way of a proposal AND a wedding date. The enemy is always looking to throw you off your target, so you have to remain diligent.

[22]Isaiah 46:10 | [23]Matthew 18:18, Luke 10:19

The Prayers of the Righteous Avail Much

After two and a half years of faithful (but not anxious) prayer for my husband, I knew his name, what he looked like, and his walk. I was immediately able to recognize him, because I had an image on paper that danced in my mind every day. It was almost as if I had known him all along. Of all the 29 characteristics that were on the list, he was 28 of them. The one he wasn't, I had written next to it, "CDW (can do without)." Did he look the way I thought he would? No. Was I disappointed? Not even a little bit. Was he anything like the men I dated before? No, thank goodness, because if he had been, then he'd end up like them—no longer a part of my life. In fact, I was so open to letting God have his way, if someone had told me how it would unfold, I wouldn't have believed him or her. Everything happened so uncharacteristically from what I was used to … but that makes sense, since what I was used to was one disappointment after another.

Two weeks after we met, and averaging 5 hours per day of talk time on the phone, I got confirmation that this was my husband. I was on the phone with him talking about how I was so frustrated at how crazy my schedule had become, and how that had really affected my personal time to read the Bible. Without missing a beat, he said, "Well, do you have your Bible nearby now? You want to do a Bible study over the phone?" I was stunned. I had met men who said they loved God, but there was never any *real*, tangible evidence. In those moments between him asking me to do Bible study and me answering the question, I had an epiphany. Suddenly, all the things I had been praying about began to rapidly reconcile in my head with all the different conversations I had with him over the previous two weeks. I knew before I said, "yes" that someday I'd be saying, "I do." Important note: I never mentioned this to him or gave him any indication of my epiphany until AFTER he proposed four months later. Timing is everything. Remember, "He who finds a wife…" from chapter 2?

If not, do a refresher read.

Keep in mind, your experience and timeframe may be—in fact—*will* be very different from mine in one way or another, because God deals with each of us according to who we are. Even when relinquishing control to God, be careful not to grab a hold of the wheel again. Three months after meeting my husband, I became overly concerned about how fast our relationship was progressing and wanted to slow things down. After all, where we had grown in our relationship after only 3 months was more like where most people are after 2 years! I started to try to figure out how I could fit us into a more common equation: date for a year or so, be engaged for a year, then get married. But when I approached him with, "I think we should slow things down," and I couldn't provide any better reason than, "because," he immediately rebuked me and said, "Who are you to tell God at what speed we should be growing?" I was silenced. At that point, I soberly released the wheel and allowed God to have control again. A month later we were engaged. Four months after that, we were married.

The bottom line is, whatever you do, don't get locked into *how* you think this process will pan out. Do, however, get locked into your commitment to God. And trust that wherever this ride goes, you'll arrive at the perfect place at the perfect time, prepared for a man that's not perfect, but perfect for you.

Action for Chapter 3

"...Write the vision and make it plain on tablets, that he may run who reads it." – Habakkuk 2:2

Write the vision and make it plain. Bring focus and clarity into the selection process by knowing what you are looking for first.

Set an hour or two aside to complete the process.

Begin with prayer, asking God to help you hear Him clearly as you compile your list.

Be still and listen. As things begin to come up, write them down on your list. The order in which they appear on the list is not as important as knowing whether it should be on the list at all.

There is no right number of attributes God would have you place on your list. You may have 6 or 30. If your list gets very long, you may want to reevaluate if you are still tuned in to God, or if you are adding your two cents in.

Once you have finished making the list, categorize a select few as "MUST have" or "MH."

Likewise, label accordingly the few that you "can do without" or "CDW."

Use this list as a guide to begin praying over your husband with thanksgiving to God, daily.

Remember, it is not necessary that your future husband be a 100% match, but that he meets most of the criteria that God has laid out for you.

Below are some scriptural references that will help you discover God's thoughts on husbands and wives:

a. Ps. 37:3-5
b. Eph. 5:22-33
c. 1 Peter 3:7
d. Colossians 3:19
e. Genesis 2:23-24; Matthew 19:3-9
f. Proverbs 5:19; Malachi 2:14-15
g. 1 Samuel 1:8
h. Genesis 31:4-7
i. 1 Corinthians 7:11,12,14,16

Chapter 4

Personal Maintenance

Now that you have a Godly vision of the man God would have for you, it's time to get down to the real work ... YOU! Doing all the necessary work to get ready for marriage without taking the time to work on yourself is like showing up to your beautiful and elaborately planned $150,000 wedding ceremony, but forgetting to buy your gown, get your hair, make-up, and nails done, and leaving the rings and vows at home. You could still go through with it, but you'd be a bride not easily forgotten—and not in a good way. You'd arrive only to find yourself grossly underprepared for the day's event.

Oftentimes, the same ol' pitfalls that we experience from one relationship to the next have little to do with the quality of men we meet or even the impact our culture has on them. More often, it has to do with us: our thinking, our beliefs, our experiences, and our discipline. It is unrealistic to believe that you could just keep doing what you've always done and expect a different result. It's also quite unfair to expect Mr. Wonderful to have all his stuff together and you can't even walk into a Wal-Mart without spending out of control on what you call, "deals too good to pass up." Now is the time to step it up and find out what you really have to offer a brother.

Self Examination

Undergoing an honest self-evaluation will be the most

difficult part of preparing for marriage, because it will force you to look within and deal with all your foul attitudes, faulty belief systems, and bad habits. These characteristics that make up your "bad and ugly" side started when you were a kid and have grown and morphed into this monster you no longer fear, but endear like a childhood "blankie." You've accepted them as, "that's just who I am" only because they have such a painful stronghold on you. The result is that you cling to them and protect them with such fierceness, because even just a little meddling causes great pain or discomfort. It's a lot like when you first start working out or begin a new exercise routine. The next day, you feel great (unless you move, of course). Unfortunately, the fastest way to get rid of the pain is to keep it moving and push through the aches and discomfort. Being still will cause the pain to be prolonged for an unnecessary amount of time, not unlike your personal and emotional makeup.

Self-examination is critical to marital preparedness.

Whatever you do, DO NOT SKIP THIS STEP in the marital preparation process. Don't just brush it under the rug and say, "I've been doing pretty good. As long as I keep it covered, it won't smell." This is a **huge** mistake! Marriage has a way of disturbing the most rotten, innermost part of you—indirectly. If you truly desire to be a better person, it's actually a benefit to you. Think of it as God's way of cleaning out your junk. If you're the kind that's resistant to change, your joy will leave you faster than you can imagine. If you don't deal with it now, the day-to-day interaction with your husband and the intimate dynamic nature of being married will begin to subtly aggravate your mess. You won't even be able to identify the cause of the stench because it will be so indirect. You will, however, notice the repeat arguments over things that seem rather insignificant, the irritation you feel at your husband's "unwillingness" to change, along with his "inability" to understand you, and a constant tug-of-war over who's right, who's in control, and whose fault it is. If you do the hard work now, you can avoid the even harder work later. And the harder work later can be so hard, statistics show that most people just bail out instead. Marriage is intense enough when both parties are ready, willing and able. Don't make it miserable by bringing your "poo" into the relationship. I know you probably think yours doesn't stink, but that's only because you're used to it. The reality is, it's probably strong enough to make a grown man fight back tears, and if you don't do something about it, you may get the opportunity to witness this yourself.

Sometimes I hear women say that they are tired of being told to enjoy their single lives now while they "still have the freedom to do what they want." And I understand the argument. At some point, you begin to feel, "Okay, God. I got this single thing down pat. I am **so** ready to move on!" Not so long ago, I was in those shoes. You know that expression, "the grass is always greener on the other side?" This is a classic example of that. The truth is, you are ready when **God** says you're ready. When He knows you can handle it, He will send your husband to you. He won't send him prematurely and set you up for failure.

If you are a woman frustrated with the advice to enjoy this time with God while you have it, this is a symptom that you are not yet ready. In order to have a marriage that is fulfilling, passionate and successful, you have to be willing and content with letting God have *total control of your life*. I'm talking, complete surrender. That means trusting God's timing in everything! It's important when you begin to feel frustrated that you redirect that energy to finding out what God wants you to work on next. There's a reason He's giving you so much time. If you use it efficiently, your time will be shorter. God is not interested in wasting your time, but sometimes we can hold up our own progress by jumping ahead of ourselves without all the necessary information. The next time you feel the urge to ask God, "When is it going to be my turn?" instead ask Him, "What do I need to do/learn next to be ready?"

When I took on this "total surrender" mindset, the doors blew wide open and things began to progress rather rapidly for me—all while fully enjoying every moment of it. Honestly, I miss that intimacy I had with God back then. He is still my first true love, but I don't have the same carefree abandon that once characterized my relationship with Him. It has grown and matured and I have had to become more skillful in maintaining the passion. And now, I prefer this higher level of communion and stewardship. I suppose the bottom line is, the grass is not greener, just different, so relax and begin to appreciate where you are.

Get to Work

Begin by taking an honest look at your past relationships—however deep or short-lived they may have been. In order for this step to be effective, you will need to be painfully honest with yourself, and maybe for the first time in your life, accept responsibility for your actions. Avoid placing the blame on your ex and take the viewpoint from a place of ownership. In other words, own up to how you contributed to the ending of that relationship. What kind of behaviors did or didn't you allow to take place? What kind of decisions did you make that ultimately led to the end of the relationship? What did you expect that you either did not and/or could not have logically received? What did you ignore? What did you blow out of proportion? Take a step back and look at it. *Stop reading and do this now.*

What common themes did you see and how can you improve

that behavior? If you don't get anything else from this book but insight on how you can be a better person, you've gained priceless wisdom and are already way ahead of most people in terms of personal growth and living up to your fullest potential.

Next, you'll want to sit down with one or two people (separately) who know you **very** well and get their opinions of you. Make sure these are people who know you in at least two different roles (i.e., as a colleague and personal friend, or relative and workout partner, or as a mother and neighbor, etc.). Find out what qualities they believe make you so wonderful and the areas where you need some real help. Encourage them to be frank and honest. Sugarcoating will only hurt you. The more honest they are, the more you'll get out of this exercise, so put on your thick skin and take notes. You knew they loved you before you asked and they'll love you the same after you ask. After all, it's not like they just came up with this stuff. They've known all along. You knowing what they think won't change that. Remember, this is *only* about you. Don't use this opportunity to tell them what you think of them now that your ego is bruised. Stay focused. What you hear is how they experience you, and you may agree or disagree. But chances are, if two different people see the same thing, it's likely something you'd want to heavily consider working on.

I clearly remember having this conversation with two dear friends of mine. One was a guy friend that I grew up with who had really seen me in every role possible. The other was a girlfriend that I met at church whom I had grown very fond of because of our similar experiences, but we had stark differences in personality. In a nutshell, one told me that I was too passive and didn't really know how to get what I wanted, and the other told me that my honesty could easily be interpreted as rudeness since it didn't seem like I took others' feelings into account when I spoke. A rude passivist ... interesting. Although I always thought of myself as someone who was very receptive to how people were responding to their environment, it was hard for me to accept responsibility for, and identify, when *I* was the one inflicting the pain. On another note, I really wasn't feeling my overachiever best friend telling me I didn't have enough "grrr" to get the things I truly wanted in life. Now, I'm still working on being aware of my frankness—and I believe it's getting better all the time—but in the face of fear, I found purpose and passion and am now pursuing it with loving aggression. I'm not saying I couldn't have done it without them, I just know it would not have been so soon. Friends and family are for more than just laughs and fun. They are essential in helping us grow.

Finally, you'll want to examine how you relate to your family and colleagues. Do you take them for granted? Do you pretend to be listening or be interested when they talk to you? Do you discount their value to the team or gossip about them behind their backs? In what areas do you do well, and where do you find the most resistance? Because you will relate to your husband on many different levels, knowing how you respond in these relationships will give you a heads up on areas you can look to improve.

Having Grace

Oftentimes, the things that bother us the most in other people are the very areas where we fall short ourselves, and that's why it bothers us so much. It reminds us where we don't quite measure up to our own standards. For this reason, we must be mindful to give grace to others, especially a potential husband. God deals with us in His own time and it's important that we don't point the finger or accuse others of being "less than" when

> *The best way to encourage others in their shortcomings is to focus on yours.*

we aren't finished yet either. This is not to say that you shouldn't heavily consider the consequence of his questionable behavior. On the contrary, seriously evaluate what kind of issues you can work through and which ones you wouldn't wish on your enemies. In other words, if he never changes, will you be okay with that behavior? This is the best time to tune in to all his imperfections. Is the questionable act a one-time mistake or a habit? Keep in mind, each of you will make mistakes and have flaws, so expect them and give grace where grace is needed. No one is perfect—and that includes you.

The best thing to do in encouraging others in their shortcomings is to put your focus on you. Trying to be their conscience by pointing out all the areas where you think they need help (either directly or indirectly) will only perpetuate the situation. Even the Bible says, "first take the plank out of your own eye, and then you will see clearly to remove the speck from your brother's eye[24]." The greatest revelation anyone can have of themselves is self-revelation: It's when you are able to identify *your own* flaws that you are most open for the most lasting impact for change. I'm not suggesting that you don't share how their actions are affecting you, only that you speak your mind, then move on.

There is not one, single thing you can do to change a person. Let me say that again. **THERE IS NOT ONE, SINGLE THING YOU CAN DO TO CHANGE ANOTHER PERSON.** Nothing! All you can do is change yourself. You are the only one you have control or power over. If you change how you react to certain things, you automatically will change how that person will respond to you. Check your motivation, though. Manipulation will cause you to change temporarily, then quit when you don't see any results. Committing to change will cause you to stick to it no matter what, because you're not doing it to get something, but to give the world around you a better version of you. Furthermore, be a catalyst by modeling the behavior you desire.

---

[24]Matthew 7:5

There are few things more contagious than a life lived well.

Law of Attraction

There's a lot to be said about the law of attraction and countless books, theories and theologies explaining how it works. I'll give you the simple version, with an example straight from the Bible.

Basically, the law of attraction says: You are who you think you are AND everyone around you agrees. Seems pretty simple, yet not everyone will be able to immediately reconcile this in their life. Sometimes, who we want to be and who we think we are, are two different things; and often, we confuse the two. Here's one way to test this theory: compare who you say you are to how you behave and how you feel people respond to you. Do they match? Is there any internal struggle? If things don't add up or if you feel somewhere inside, you are still trying to convince yourself of who you are, chances are pretty high that you aren't living up to your potential.

In the 13th chapter of the book, Numbers, God tells Moses to send in a group of men to survey Canaan, the land God had promised to give them. God told them that it was a land flowing with milk and honey and that the fruit was good. Sounds great, right? But when the men returned, they said that although what God had said was true, there were also giants in the land, and since these men saw themselves as grasshoppers in their own eyes, the giants also saw them as such. As a result, God condemned them never to enter into Canaan all because they didn't see themselves as God saw them and cowered away in fear. The bottom line is, if deep down you don't feel worthy, you won't be, because you will subconsciously act as such, causing others to agree with what you believe. If you don't see the value, no one else will either.

Take an active approach in strengthening how you see yourself and you'll begin to attract people who are worthy of your company, and likewise. In Proverbs 23:7, it says, "for as [a person] thinks in his heart, so is he." Who is it you want to be? Find several ways to begin to display those attributes and start acting like the woman you want to become. Maybe you want to be a woman of her word. If so, begin to follow through on your commitments and be realistic about what you can accomplish in a set amount of time. Also, if you can't complete a commitment in the agreed timeframe, explain your situation *before* you default on the agreement. Doing so preserves your integrity and allows room for the other party to make the necessary adjustments (provided this isn't your regular mode of operation).

Perhaps you want to be more giving. Start actively looking for opportunities to give of your resources: your time, your money, and your talents. Maybe you'll want to start carrying around an extra $100 bill to give away at will, or you'll start volunteering your time at your church or in your community. You could even offer your much needed talent to a relevant non-profit organization.

Take control of your circumstances by thinking good thoughts.

If you are not exactly sure where to start, you can find numerous Christian books that speak of the promises of God and who God has created us to be. Of course, you could always go straight to the source and find it for yourself in the Bible. There are many examples of how God thinks of you in scripture. For example, God says you are fearfully and wonderfully made and that your worth is far more than rubies[25]. If you don't believe it yet, tell yourself in the mirror every day until you do. However it is that you want to be perceived, start walking in it daily, and as soon as it becomes habit, others will recognize it in you, too.

Finally, combat negative thoughts. If you can grab a hold

---

[25]Psalm 139:14, Proverbs 31:10 | [26]Luke 6:45

of this exercise, you'll cause a domino effect of great things to happen in your life. Philippians 4:8 says, "whatever is true, whatever is noble, whatever is right, whatever is pure, whatever is lovely, whatever is admirable—if anything is excellent or praiseworthy—think about such things." The more you think about these things, the faster they get into your heart. Out of the abundance of your heart, you'll begin to speak those things[26]. We've known since we were kids, "what you say is what you get." But what we didn't know until we got older and someone showed us in the Bible, is that this is actually true. Once you begin to speak those things, you'll cause them to manifest, since the words you speak have the ability to bring life and death[27]. Don't think or speak yourself right out of your blessing. Raise your awareness and be intentional about saying positive things out loud. YES, you *do* deserve it! Take control of your circumstances, control of who you are and who you want to be by thinking good thoughts. Imagine the possibilities in that.

The Ultimate Purpose

It is important to understand that the ultimate purpose of all this personal maintenance is so that you can create a strong union with your future husband that God can actually use. Having your needs met and being fulfilled is not the purpose of marriage, but a byproduct of it. *The primary purpose of marriage is to develop a relationship that most resembles the love Christ has for us.* In doing so, we exercise all the major discipleship muscles by walking in love, forgiveness, understanding, service, honor, and holiness. The more exercise we get, the stronger we become. The stronger we become, the more God can use us to bless His people, and the more He can entrust to us. In case you missed it, that means more favor for you. If you've never experienced God's favor, it's a lot like someone going ahead of you everyday making

---

[27]Proverbs 18:21

sure the best opportunities and the best outcome in every moment of your day is set up for you. Truly, there's nothing like it.

Marriage is the perfect workout to become the best person you can possibly be, and one of the most hands-on ways of becoming more like Christ, each and every day. If you take personal maintenance seriously, and spend time every so often reevaluating where you are, you will experience God's abundance not only in your future marriage relationship, but also with every relationship in your life.

Action for Chapter 4

" ... first take the plank out of your own eye, and then you will see clearly to remove the speck from your brother's eye." – *Matthew 7:5*

Are you ready to roll up your sleeves? I hope so, because while this may be some of the most challenging work for you to do, it is also the most rewarding. Take this action a bit slow to get maximum benefit, rereading the chapter if necessary. Compromised integrity = a compromised marriage, so the key is not to get it all done at once just to say "it's done," but to fully commit to change. It's better to commit to and perfect one thing, than it is to haphazardly rush through 7 things and have none of it stick.

Here are a few pointers to get you going in the right direction:

If you haven't done so already, begin to assess all your past romantic relationships and your relationships with family, friends, and colleagues. From the perspective of personal responsibility (how your contributions and decisions affected the relationship), ask yourself and answer the following questions:

- How did you contribute to the ending of that relationship?
- What kind of behaviors did or didn't you allow to take place?
- What kind of decisions did you make that ultimately led to the end of the relationship?
- What did you expect that you either did not and/or could not have logically received?
- What did you ignore?
- What did you blow out of proportion?
- Based on the effort you put forth, do you feel like you did the best you knew how?
- If you could change anything about the relationships you

have with your friends and family (thinking of specific relationships), what would it be? What can you do about it?

- What common themes do you see?

Select two people who both know you well in a couple of different roles and love you enough to be honest with you. Put on thick skin and ask them to give you an honest assessment of yourself: the good—and more importantly—the bad. Take notes and review them in your own private time. Which ones can you see, now that someone has pointed them out to you? What can you do to improve that area?

Begin to walk in the greatness God has called you to by acting like the person you want to become. Choose one character quality and begin practicing it.

Become aware of your own negativity and combat those thoughts and words with positivity.

Chapter 5

Do Your Homework

If you're like me, the mere thought of having homework to do instantly makes you want to shrink and disappear until the coast is clear. I admit it, I could've been a much better student in my schooled years if back then I could comprehend the justification and benefit of homework. Now as an adult, I fully understand its purpose: to help me learn what I was taught, so that it sticks long after I leave the classroom. Understanding the "why" as *well* as being in the right frame of mind really makes a difference in how effective homework actually is. Although honestly, I'm not sure knowing would've made a difference for me as a teenager, unless of course, someone could've shown me a picture of myself in college struggling with calculus because my study habits were so poor. They say, "the third time's a charm," but frankly, there's nothing charming about business calculus. I was just happy to get out of there alive.

Similarly, if someone could show you a glimpse of how miserable your marriage would be 10 years down the road because you didn't do your homework or you didn't do it with a value-added mindset, you may see it as less of a burden and more of a genuine desire. While the consequence of not doing your homework in school may have been attending summer school for a few weeks, the consequence of not doing your homework before getting married could lead to years of pain, heartache, broken homes, shattered dreams, bitterness, multiple divorces, and the list goes on and on.

Think in these terms, if a person has to study medicine for 8 – 10 years and pass an exam before they can become a doctor who will eventually retire, how much more important is it that you study with the same intensity to be a wife, who not only cannot retire, but is vowing to stay committed "until death do you part"? If you are committing yourself to something that is going to last the rest of your life, shouldn't you know a thing or two about it *and* be good at it? It's confusing to me how two people can pretty much meet on the bus one afternoon, and if they really hit it off, can get a license to get married the same day. There are literally NO requirements for obtaining a marriage license in California except that you're a legal adult and not already married. Teenagers MUST complete so many hours of drivers' training and education before they can get a driver's license, because otherwise, they put the lives of innocent people at risk. Isn't it just as risky for those entering into marriage? The stakes are just as high for married people, but so far, there's nothing in place to protect the innocent when marriages go awry because of ill training and lack of preparation.

Thankfully in this age, there is an abundance of resources you can tap into to get the training and knowledge needed to make the most of your marriage, and to protect the lives of the ones you love most. Unfortunately, taking an active part in those resources is pretty unpopular and is seen as rather unimportant.

Educate Yourself

Keep your eyes and ears open for seminars, conferences, and classes for singles *and* married people, and attend as many as you can, with caution. Don't shy away from seminars for married people unless being married is a requirement. It is much better to get the information you need before you get married, than it is to get married and be in need of wisdom that you now have to go out and find. Be sure that the material that is being presented is sound and not gimmicky, trendsetting, or new age. There's really nothing new under the sun[28]. Remember, God created the institute of marriage at the beginning of time. All the basic principles you'll need to have success as a wife are pretty ancient. Notice I said *principles*, not *rules*. Rules are subjective and open to perceived interpretation. They create an atmosphere of compliance rather than agreement, and where there's no agreement, there's no conviction; hence the saying, "rules are meant to be broken." Furthermore, rules are for games and marriage is definitely NOT a game. Games have winners and losers. No matter how fair you play, there is no way for you to 1) ensure that you win, while you 2) prevent the other from losing. Furthermore, in games, you are required to keep score and nothing ruins a marriage faster than a scorekeeper.

Practice principles, not rules.

Begin reading marriage material on a variety of topics and measure it against a solid standard—the Bible. Know that not everything you read will be useful or correct. Use your filtering system (that we'll discuss more in a moment) to extract the good. Everything else that contradicts the Word of God and is unreliable, throw it out. Once you have the good information, turn it into knowledge by studying. Take notes, highlight, use imagery or whatever you need to do to get the information from your eyes, to your brain. Once you have the knowledge, you can turn it into wisdom by applying it in your life in practical situations. For the most part, you'll be learning how to submit in a relationship and be considerate of others while maintaining who you are as a priceless jewel. You don't need a husband to practice these things, just friends and family you love.

This step of practical application is vitally important, not just

[28]Ecclesiastes 1:9

here, but in any area of your life where you want to grow. Knowledge alone doesn't enhance your life, but experiencing knowledge does. ***YOU HAVE TO DO SOMETHING***. Not taking action on what you learn (which is the same as deciding to do nothing) is a declaration saying that you are okay with the way things are now. You can't read this or any book and say that it didn't change your life if you didn't do anything with the information you consumed. Information is like a tool, a hammer, let's say. Just having a hammer does you no good until you pick it up and begin to use it to hit the head of a nail. Suddenly, you have progress. Be diligent and DO what you learn. Don't just sit on the information. You'll never experience significance in anything by doing nothing.

Inquiring Minds Want to Know

Use this "in the meantime" experience to ask other women, whom you have good relationships with, about their marriage experiences. As the saying goes, "Experience is a great teacher," but I believe there are times when other people's experiences are even better than our own. Good or bad, happily married or divorced. No one is a bad example in this arena. If you know a woman whom you admire and whose marriage you admire, ask her about what she thinks is at the core of their success. Ask how they got through tough times (everyone's had them) and what they do to keep the love alive. If you know a woman who's been divorced, once or more, ask her where she thinks things went wrong. You'd be amazed at how honest and open women are when talking to someone they both love and trust. Many times they are willing to share what they learned so that you won't have to experience the

> *The experiences of others can be an even better teacher than our own.*

[29]Titus 2:3-5

same thing[29]. Listen to what she says and what she *doesn't* say. Just by implementing this exercise, I learned how to properly transition into a blended family, how to avoid divorce and how to guard off infidelity. I learned some things I can do to stay connected with my husband amid busyness and how to safeguard our relationship. As with all resources of information, balance what's said with what you know God says. If she tells you she keeps love alive by having a honey on the side, then your discernment should perk up and tell you that's a recipe for trouble. Which leads me to the next area of concern …

Qualify people who give you advice. People will give you unsolicited advice regarding marriage and how you should go about it. Of course they mean well, they just don't always know well. Before you allow someone to speak into your life or before you receive what they have to say, check their fruit. How does what they tell you show up in their life, if at all? Do they live what they preach? Does what they say originate from fear? Are they speaking to you from a personal experience or divine wisdom? Personal experience says, "When you get married, make sure you have some money on the side, because if he ever leaves you (like So-and-so's husband did her), you won't be left with nothing." Divine wisdom says, "When you get married, make sure you know that God is your provider, protector, and sustainer and that He approves of your mate." Be weary of anyone who says, they "know what the Bible says, **but** … I think x-y-z." A person who thinks they know better than God is a dangerous person to confide in[30].

Your Sixth Sense

It will be of great benefit to you at this time to begin to develop your sense of discernment. Your discernment is basically your ability to judge well, using prompts from the Holy Spirit. Some call this their "gut" feeling or intuition. Spending time with God and/or praying in the spirit will edify you inwardly and make you more sensitive

[30]Proverbs 10:17, 27; 11:14; 24:6

to the voice of God. As you begin to train your ear to hear from Him and your spirit to feel for Him, He will reveal things to come and give you insight into your current situations. As previously discussed, it will also act as a filtering system helping you to pull the truth out of situations more easily. There are no shortcuts, though. This only begins to happen when you spend time with Him[31].

If you are using this book properly and actually doing the action steps, you may have already noticed a heightened awareness in your discernment now that you have been spending more time with God, getting to know Him. This sixth sense proves to be a priceless tool when it comes to identifying a potential husband. In the two years that I spent preparing for my husband, my sense of discernment was so strong, that when men approached me, I knew within a matter of a couple minutes whether or not he was worth my time. I can hear all the sisters saying, "What I wouldn't have done to have *that* skill before I started dating the last loser."

It is a process that takes time to develop, but you'll never regret that you did. Soon you may find that hearing from God is the easy part. The real sign of growth is when you can hear Him AND you obey what He's telling you to do.

No Wo-man is an Island

One of the biggest helps to me in this stage was having support. Knowing there were other women that I could turn to for advice and encouragement, really helped keep me focused on who God was calling me to be as a wife and a virtuous woman. It helps if you have a friend or mentor who will reason with you from a place that you can trust (the Bible), and not lose her sense of integrity because she's caught up in your drama or because she doesn't want to hurt your feelings. There may be times when you'll want to go back to your old way of doing things, but having that support will help you through the

[31] 1 Corinthians 2:14; Philippians 1:9-11; Hebrews 4:12

fog and remind you of the results you got when you did things your way[32]. Remember, if you absolutely insist on your own way, God will not stop you, but don't expect him to bless your disobedience either[33].

For some of you, connecting with other women and being vulnerable to them is extremely uncomfortable. I know. I used to be one of those women. Back then, I'd rather beat my head against a wall than open up to a woman about my most intimate concerns. Because of experiences that left me feeling disenchanted and the cattiness of other young ladies around me as I was coming into womanhood, I withdrew complete trust from the entire gender! Everyone was a potential backstabber as far as I was concerned, so for years, I wouldn't let another woman get too close.

It wasn't until several years after becoming a mother that I began to yearn for that fellowship with a woman friend that only women understand. Then, the more I began to read and grow as a Christian, the more I began to see what was happening. Ever since the beginning with Adam and Eve in the Garden of Eden, sin and corrupt spirits have been at work to destroy what God has created. Part of that plan for women has been a "divide and conquer" strategy. If Satan can keep up enough strife between women, then he can break down the amazing strength we have when we stand together. If you've never read about it, there is an amazing story of such in the book of Ruth, in the Bible. It's a dynamic account of what can happen when women support each other with the love of God. As elementary as it may seem, women communicate in ways that resonate with other women. We have similar experiences and process information in similar ways. And while **there is no better match for a woman than a man,** having women

Secrets create bondage, but disclosure is truly freeing.

---

[32]Proverbs 27:17; James 5:16 | [33]Proverbs 13:13

friends will remind you that you are not alone and you are not crazy.

Still, you won't be able to trust everyone, but using discernment, you'll be able to find a woman friend who will have your back and support you through it all. It has been the openness and willingness to share on the part of my women friends and family that I have grown into the wife I am today. Secrets keep you in bondage, but disclosure is truly freeing—not only to you—but to other women as well. I believe that if more women took a chance and opened up to just one other woman, women relations would improve and marriages as a whole would be more successful as we learn from one another.

Study, Study, Study

When you read material on being single and preparing for marriage, or when you go to seminars and classes, take the information seriously. Let it really get into you. You will be tested on what you've learned every day with people already in your life, and the *final* comes when you get married. It's ongoing and lasts day after day. You don't want to go into the final without spending a sufficient amount of time studying. The consequence is far worse than a bad grade. It's a bad marriage. You can gauge your performance throughout the process by looking at your fruit: how do your children view marriage? What does your husband say about you? What's the condition of your relationship? Can you teach other women what you've learned? Better yet, are you learning something? These are all questions you will need to encounter once you get married. The answers depend on how well you prepare for the final.

Action for Chapter 5

"my people are destroyed from lack of knowledge ..." – *Hosea 4:6*

If you are too freaked out by the idea of being assigned "homework," think of this as an opportunity to expand your relationship I.Q.

Read one book a month or read 30 minutes a day of material that will make you a better wife. If reading is really hard for you, most books can be purchased as audio books on CD or can be downloaded to your computer or mp3 player.

- Choose a range of topics from marriage to parenting to finances to what men need and how they're created to think.

Over the next 3 months, look for classes or seminars in your area (or abroad if you love to travel) on being married or singleness as it relates to preparing for marriage. Commit to attend 1 or 2 that interest you.

DO THE WORK from the classes/seminars you attend.

Create your network of women friends.

- Intentionally set time aside to spend with other women building relationships and developing support.
- Reconnect with old friends and be a support to someone else.

Read the book of Ruth in the Bible. It is a powerful story of how when women stick together, they are able to usher in blessings that exceed imagination.

Chapter 6

Purpose Produces Passion

After all the hype died down, thc price dropped, and they worked out most of the bugs, my husband and I decided to get this new, all touch screen, smart phone. The manufacturer claimed that the phone was so easy to use, you could just pick it up and start using it with no instructions or demo. They were so confident with this claim, in fact, that there was no manual or quick-start flyer of any kind included with the phone. All that came in the box was the phone, a USB cord, charger, earphones and a cleaning cloth. Initially, I had no complaints. I could easily figure out the basic functions on the phone just by relating back to my former smart phone.

Weeks later, I was listening to a podcast with the earphones using the mp3 feature on my phone. Suddenly, the podcast was interrupted by an incoming call that was transmitted through the earphones. Unbeknownst to me, the earphones weren't just for the mp3 player, but doubled as a hands-free earpiece. Now, in my defense, I was not born in the technology era, so I may have missed a few perceived assumptions. But this was actually great news to me because I was in need of a hands-free device, but had never noticed there was a tiny microphone attached to the cord, which would have been a telltale sign for me.

Not long after the value of my phone increased for me with this new discovery, I found myself utterly frustrated. Whenever I used the earphones with phone calls, if I moved the cord a certain way, the call would disconnect. It wasn't until several "dropped" calls later that I realized if I applied just a small amount of pressure to the microphone, there was a mechanism inside that, with a tiny click, would voluntarily end my call. It wasn't long before I found out this minute mechanism could also answer calls and start and stop the mp3 feature. Once I figured this all out (and who knows what else I still don't know), my phone was more useful to me than ever!

You can greatly increase your value by tapping into your purpose.

Here's my point: had I never realized the phone's true potential with the earphones, I probably would've been okay even though the results were not impressive. But, knowing its purpose and capabilities greatly improved *my* productivity *and* its worth to me. In the very same manner, you can greatly increase your own self-worth and value to others by tapping into your purpose and passions and walking in them with confidence.

Do the Math

Marriage is a very unique union that involves some very interesting math. In the book of Mark, chapter 10:5-8, it says

> *... God made male and female to be together. Because of this, a man leaves father and mother, and in marriage he becomes one flesh with a woman—no longer two individuals, but forming a new unity ... (The Message translation)*

That's right, 1 + 1 = 1. Only God has the authority to change facts and still end up with a true statement. Here's where you'll need to pay close attention: it doesn't say two parts make a whole. It says two *wholes* make a whole. Are you with me? In other words, if you don't really know who you are and anticipate finding that one person who makes you feel whole, you are *in* the hole (so to speak). You'll be entering into a relationship with an emotional and mental deficit, and if you marry someone with the same focus, you're really going to be in trouble!

If you're looking for someone to make you feel whole, you're in the hole.

Don't get caught up in la-la movie land, like in that scene from *Jerry McGuire* where Jerry (Tom Cruise) looks at Dorothy (Renee Zellweger), and in his desperate attempt to win her back, humbly says, "You complete me." A tearjerker, I'm sure, but that's stuff made for movies—not real life. If you need another person to complete you, you are in bad shape, because someone else is only human and **will** disappoint you. Think about it. What happens if that person goes away or dies an untimely death? Are you now incomplete again? Isn't that a sad place to be, when the sum of your own self-worth and value are dependent upon the performance and presence of another well-meaning, yet guaranteed-to-be-faltering human being? This is called codependency, and it doesn't matter where you look this definition up, it's not a good thing. God puts high value on relationships, and depending on one another, but codependency is an excessive emotional or psychological dependency on another person that often has associations like an addiction. Too much of anything is bad for you, so if you feel you may need a 12-step program in codependency, start by digging up the treasure (which is your purpose) that is already imbedded inside of you. If you feel you have a serious problem, there is no shame in getting professional help. In fact, it's wisdom.

Maximize Your Value

Here's how to get the most out of life *and* give the most out of life: Know your purpose. Every human walking the earth was created for a purpose unique to that individual. None of us were created to just … be. God is not a haphazard thinker. Just like Jeremiah, before you were formed in your mother's womb, He knew you. You were not an accident. And although you may have been a surprise for your parents, you were fully thought out, planned and filled with a specific purpose, for this specific time, by the Master Creator Himself. Until you know what your purpose is **and** begin to walk in it, there are countless people (including yourself) waiting for you, suffering because you have something they need.

Anytime you don't fully understand why something was created, you are at risk of misusing that thing. Your purpose is no different. If you don't understand what your purpose is, you may dedicate 20 years to saving the whales when you were suppose to be saving the art programs in public schools. Both are noble causes, but only one has you operating at your maximum potential; therefore, only one of them creates the most value for your life and makes you feel truly alive. This is what you owe the world: you at your maximum potential, and if you don't see it yet, there is nothing more appealing or attractive than a woman who embodies the full essence of who she is.

Don't make the mistake of identifying what you do as a living with what your purpose is. Your purpose is *who* you are, not *what* you do. My individual purpose is to strengthen marriages, and my assignment is to encourage and prepare women for marriage. I may write, teach, speak, or mentor as a way of living out my purpose. However, my purpose is not to *be* a teacher, a speaker, a mentor, or even a mother or a wife, because any one of these titles can be taken away from me in a number of unfortunate circumstances, at which point, I would be left without a purpose. Your purpose is what's inside of you, written on your heart, and it can never be taken away.

Knowing your purpose and being one with it provides a multitude of benefits. Just to name a few, it:

a. Gives your life direction. When you know what it is you were created to do, you no longer waste your time doing things for the sake of "the good," but for "goodness' sake." There is no greater good than giving the world what no one else could produce. It's easier to make up your mind when you have tough decisions to make because one option will line up with your purpose, the other will not.

b. Builds confidence and self-value. When you realize that there is not one single person who can do what you do with quite the same flair **and** you understand that God created *you* to do it, because He knew the world needed it, you can stick out your chest a bit—as long as you remember you can only do what you do because of God.

c. Adds fulfillment. Finally, you can see the difference and the impact you are making in the world, and it brings you joy to be able to give back what God has so graciously deposited in you.

d. Protects you. As long as you are following God's purpose for your life, God will protect your life until your mission is accomplished. In all that Jesus faced, not once did He fear premature death, because He knew His purpose, and He knew His end. Jesus knew as long as He served the Father, His life would end just as God had planned. In Mark 8:31, Jesus gave his disciples an account of his impending death. And despite what the disciples saw as a grim outlook, Jesus knew, in that fulfilling His purpose, He'd give us the ultimate gift of salvation and He'd receive the highest reward of all, a seat at God's right hand.

Divorce Repellant

If you haven't uncovered your purpose or assignment yet, now is the time. Knowing will protect you from a variety of marital ailments that tend to occur once the newness of matrimony wears off, and you get isolated from the distractions of rearing children, building careers, and managing the "heavy duties" in life. Often during the courting stages, people willingly conform to the likes and dislikes of their desired counterpart—not because they necessarily agree—but because they don't know what else to do or don't have a view of their own on a particular matter. Besides, it makes for joyful "life planning" if you both agree on most things. The consequence of this blind conformation is that as you grow and mature as individuals and a couple, you eventually begin to form opinions and outlooks of your own, and unfortunately, there's no guarantee that what you believe now in your maturity will line up with what you chose to go along with early on. Now you feel unfulfilled in this relationship, living a life you don't love and don't even know how you got here. At this point, most people tend to think somehow they've "fallen out of love," or that they've "made a mistake by rushing into things," or the most infamous, that they've "grown apart." This is where you find "irreconcilable differences" in legal divorce papers. One scenario that can take place when you don't really know what you want to do with your life, is that you may agree to be a stay-at-home mom (for example) only to recognize 7 years later that God has placed a burning desire in you to travel abroad as a missionary. Chances are incredibly high that when you take this piece of information to your husband, he's not going to be excited about it. He has every right to feel betrayed and be disappointed because that is not what he signed up for. Hopefully he can learn to love it, but if he can't, the future ahead begins to look quite uncertain. All of these issues are entirely preventable just by knowing your purpose.

When you know your purpose, you open the doors to an

abundantly productive partnership with your husband (or husband-to-be) and instantly have more to offer than any other "Jane" walking down the street. Right up front, he can identify whether you complement or hinder the vision he has in his heart. He doesn't have to wonder what you'll be like in 5 or 10 years or be afraid of the uncertainties. You knowing your purpose will eliminate some of the guess work in life by acting like a navigation system, constantly keeping you on track. If you complement the vision, he now sees you as an asset, and his desire to protect you and invest in you becomes top priority. If you are boldly walking in your purpose and he doesn't see the benefit, it is because your purposes don't line up—not because you don't have value. This is something you want to know long before you invest any length of time in the relationship, let alone marriage.

When both you and your partner know your purposes, or are at least working towards the revelation, you begin to see the true purpose of marriage. Suddenly, marriage becomes so much bigger than just getting your needs met, having children and having someone to snuggle with at night (although these are great byproducts of a healthy marriage). Soon you'll see that *another purpose of marriage is for God to use the two of you as a team to accomplish something significant in His kingdom.* The two of you create a spiritual synergy that can accomplish exponentially more than you could if you were working alone. Not only that, but because you realize that God brought you together for reasons much bigger than yourself, you can now see with clarity that some of the most difficult times you'll have with your husband are necessary in refining you both to produce character that is stronger, more mature, and more honorable, so that you are successful at accomplishing greatness. It is not necessarily a sign that you are no longer right for one another, but rather that God wants to stretch you and grow you so you can go to the next level. This is also an opportune time to deepen your relationship with God. When you have the integrity to stick together through the hard times, and you come out on the other side of victory, your relationship will be stronger and closer than ever before.

Excavating You

Discovering your purpose can take a few minutes or several years, depending on how you go about the process. Understand that your purpose is not something outside of yourself. You were born with your purpose already implanted inside of you. You don't have to start trying all kinds of different things to find out what you like best. You don't have to go along with what someone else thinks your purpose is. You don't have to live up to the expectation of your parents or a certain standard in society or your culture. You only have to inquire the wisdom of your Creator, God, and ask yourself a few pertinent questions. Once you have confirmation of the revelation and you begin to walk in it, doors will begin to open for you in ways you had never imagined. No longer do the standard assumptions apply.

If your purpose is to inspire people through music, you do not have to reside with the stereotype of being a "struggling artist." God's plans for you are to prosper you, not harm you—and this gift he has blessed you with will not bring you sorrow, but add richness to your life[34]. You may still experience fear and there will be obstacles, but knowing your purpose gives you the faith you need to push past both of these to gain priceless rewards.

True passion only comes from God.

If you don't know your purpose or are unsure of your purpose, do not advance to the next chapter until you have completed the exercises and have some knowledge of the direction

[34]Jeremiah 29:11, Proverbs 10:22

in which God's path for your life leads.

Igniting Passion

Finally, know that passion and purpose go hand-in-hand. When you have a true revelation of your purpose, you won't be surprised to find out that it's something you feel passionately about. But in order to sustain that passion and not get discouraged, understand that true passion only comes from God. Many people exhibit blind passion, giving something their all without really knowing the origin, and therefore, making great decisions for the wrong reasons. They may find themselves angry, frustrated, or confused throughout their pursuit of purpose because they are disconnected from The Source of their passion. The passion that He placed in you works like a battery. It is the very thing that drives you to wake up in the morning, and until you use it up, it will continue to motivate you to *give* more out of life and therefore *get* more out of life.

On the other hand, ignoring it locks up the flow of potential, causing a build up of pressure that manifests itself as dissatisfaction with life, depression, boredom, and lifelessness. You can put a dream on hold temporarily, but not your purpose. Be careful not to confuse the two. Dreams are icing on the cake of purpose. For example, my purpose is to prepare, strengthen, and encourage women in fulfilling, God-honoring marriages. But my dream may be to run a yearly international conference in three different countries catering to women who have a heart for God-honoring marriages. Do I skip purpose because I don't have the funds and resources for the dream? NO! I do what I can now, with what I have until the dream can manifest. You can still operate at full potential while your dream is on hold. But if you put your purpose on hold as well, you will operate at little to no potential and will constantly be at odds with your deepest desires. If you feel somehow that your purpose will prevent you from taking care of the basic necessities in life, you've missed the point. Your purpose will make a way for you and the passion that is released from being in purpose will open doors for you and give favor to the situations that concern you. Knowing God and allowing yourself to be refined and redirected as He sees fit guarantees your progression, success, and impact as you go forth in the Power far greater than yourself.

Releasing your passion results in a zeal for life that is not only exhilarating, but creates an energy that ignites inspiration in others. You suddenly become far more attractive and more desirable to be around because you make other people feel more alive. Looking good catches the eye, but couple that with vigor for life and you've just become a woman who is amazingly unforgettable as well.

Action for Chapter 6

"Many are the plans in a man's heart, but it is the LORD's purpose that prevails." –Proverbs 19:21

Be self-conscious—in a positive way. Set time aside to take a personal inventory of your gifts, talents, and passions.

Use the questionnaire located in Appendix 2 to help guide yourself to the discovery of your purpose.

Once you've uncovered a theme, begin to refine the details until you arrive at a specific purpose. Explore the possibilities until you find the perfect fit.

Recommended reading, *The Power of Purpose and Vision* by Dr. Myles Munroe.

Chapter 7

Sex & Lust 101

Now that you've been on this journey for a while of preparing yourself for marriage, have you given any thought to what you'd like to give your new husband as a wedding gift? Think it's too early to be thinking about that? The reality is, the sooner you think about it, the better it gets, because the best gift you could ever give him is sexual purity. If you are still a virgin, you have the best gift to offer of all: exclusive rights to your body and affections—pure, untainted, uncharted, and in its most immaculate condition. A man's perfect dream! If you're not a virgin, you still have time to make a difference. You can make a decision today to recommit yourself to a life of sexual purity (that's code for celibacy).

When I was married, I fell into the latter category. In fact, I was a single mom. I didn't have a very lengthy sexual past, but there had certainly been more than one. When I rededicated my life to Christ, I decided I wanted to start doing things God's way and become celibate. While, for me, the *decision* was very easy, the *process* of quitting was quite another thing. In fact, it took nearly a year from the time I made the decision, to the last time I actually had sex before I was married. Personally, it was a very hard and excruciating time. That year was the lowest year of my life. There I was, involved with a man I NEVER intended—or even wanted—to marry. In fact, I didn't even really like who he was as a person, but there was a spirit of lust present that made its way to me and I literally felt like an addict. I didn't want to do what I was doing, but I couldn't find the strength to stop. Finally after months of trying to make good on my promise, it all came to a dramatic end. In the midst of the act, I suddenly began to cry uncontrollably. I pushed him off me and fell to my knees on the floor, weeping and asking God to forgive me. That day I left and asked him to never contact me again, and that was the last I saw or heard of him. God sealed that chapter in my life and restored my purity, and to God I am eternally grateful.

What I didn't understand then, but I understand now is that I was under attack. Demonic strongholds were discouraging me from doing the very thing that would bring both God and me the greatest pleasure. Sure, I could've resorted to, "I just can't help myself. It's natural," but something on the inside of me knew that there was something greater on the other side. Had I not had Jesus in my life, I don't know if I would've won the battle. That whole year, I never missed a Wednesday Bible study or a Sunday service. I know some people run *from* God when they are doing wrong, but I knew as long as I kept running *to* God, I had a lifeline to get out of it. I knew I was going to need the grace of God to help me through it. It took everything within me (plus a little more) to break free from the bondage that kept me from experiencing sex as The Creator of it intended.

Don't underestimate the power of accountability.

If you are ready to commit yourself to a life of sexual purity, but have not already enlisted a support group, you will absolutely need one now. The main reason why things became so terrible for me after making the decision to become celibate is that I didn't have a support circle in place to help me through and hold me accountable. You don't have to go through what I did. You can set yourself up for success by confiding in people who love you and support the decision you've made. Being vulnerable to someone makes all the world of difference in the level of your success. Don't underestimate the power of accountability.

Proud of my victory, I had been celibate nearly 5 years (with the exception of one mishap a year into the decision) the day I married my husband (who by the way, had also been celibate for over 4 years). Because we had both made the commitment to celibacy before meeting one another, we were able to honor God *and* ourselves throughout our courtship. While it wasn't always easy, it was always deliberate. We had several safeguards in place:

a. We almost never spent time alone. Whenever we were together, we were with our children. In the extremely rare case when the children were not with us, we were with friends or in a public place. The only time I recall us being alone in private was the day he proposed to me, and on that morning, our time alone together was short and filled with the activity of preparing a meal together.

b. We never slept under the same roof. When I went to Michigan with him for three days to meet his parents, we had reserved a hotel room for me where I could sleep uncompromised. Only because his mother insisted, the second night, I slept at his parents' home, but he slept in the detached garage out back that had a bedroom, still keeping our boundaries of not sleeping under the same roof. If I was at his place until the kids and/or I were sleepy or asleep, he'd let me stay at his place for the night because I lived an hour away and he'd sleep in his truck! Talk about commitment. Even the kids were shocked that he'd go to such lengths, but they also learned that just because something is inconvenient, that doesn't give you the right to compromise.

c. When the kids were sleep and we could steal a kiss, that's all we stole. We were very careful not to kiss too long, too passionately, or touch each other in any place that would be inappropriate to expose in public.

d. We didn't spend a lot of time being affectionate, hugging, and holding hands. We realized that the more time we spent in one another's personal space, the closer we wanted to get.

e. We talked openly about our boundaries and notified the other if something was too much or needed modifying.

Taking these precautions helped us not only keep our word, but prevented us from being in tempting situations.

On our wedding night, although neither of us were virgins, we were still able to celebrate that newness with one another and receive the blessing (or "wedding gift" as I like to call it) that God gives a husband and wife on their wedding night. We had something to be excited about, and I don't have to tell you that of all the gifts we got for our wedding, the one God gave us that night was not only superior to everything else (including my amazing salad spinner), but even today, it continues to give and give and keeps getting better all the time. I know, because I've been on both sides, the benefits you get from waiting to be sexually intimate **far** outweigh the benefits you *think* you're getting by indulging prematurely. Premarital sex doesn't secure or intensify your relationship on any meaningful level. It only gives the illusion of doing so. In fact, it does the opposite, but we'll discuss that more in a bit.

Premarital sex doesn't secure or intensify your relationship on any meaningful level.

God's Gift to the Married

Here's another way to look at it: we know that God created the institute of marriage at the beginning of mankind with Adam and Eve. *Within marriage*, He also created sex. Sex is a wonderful act of intimacy, commitment, procreation and just pure joy. Think of it as His wedding gift to you.

Do you remember being a kid at Christmas time? I do, and I also remember learning a very valuable lesson. One year I got a little curious and went searching the house for the unwrapped gifts. When I found them, I remember peeking inside and seeing all sorts of things for me and my brothers and sister. I didn't spend a lot of time surveying all the contents, but I remember having a feeling of excitement, guilt, and relief all at once. When I was done looking, I closed the bag up, just how I found it, and didn't see those things again until Christmas morning. Then the morning came that I had been anticipating for weeks, but when I opened my gifts, not only was I not excited, but I also felt like I had been robbed of joy as I tried to pretend to be happy and surprised about each gift. Since I was not enjoying the act of opening my own gifts, I looked to be entertained by my siblings, only to find that I was underwhelmed at what they received for presents as well. I just couldn't find any real joy in the spirit of Christmas. It was quite possibly my worst experience as a kid.

Sex is like those Christmas gifts. If you open them and use them before you're supposed to, what real joy do you have when someone wraps them back up and gives them to you on Christmas? By that time, you've already lost your appreciation for the gifts, and it's hardly as exciting as it was when your adrenaline was flowing and you were sneaking around trying to see what's come in since the last shopping trip. As with marriage, the gift of sex can be used prematurely, and by the time you get married, there's nothing new under the sun and nothing more to look forward to. Now all that's left is downhill, and that disappointment from the lack of sexual excitement post-matrimony turns into an undetectable cancer in your marriage. If you're patient, you can expect more than just being excited on your wedding night. Unlike Christmas, when you wait to open **this** gift when it's mature, the excitement can last a lifetime, recreating itself, and evolving over time to keep the fire alive.

Thanks, but No Thanks?

I know for some, this may seem like something that was great for me, but you don't think you could really "be down" with making a huge change like celibacy. We live in an era that is so into liberation that we have actually become imprisoned by it and don't even realize it. We, as a society, feel that anyone telling us what to do with our bodies is a violation of our right to choose. But I've learned that it's knowing and abiding in our boundaries and the boundaries of others where we truly find freedom. By following rules, we know what to expect of ourselves and others and the consequences if we don't follow those rules. Right now, no one is talking about the consequences of not following God's commandments for sexual purity, but they exist all around.

Not that long ago, I was watching television around 7 o'clock in the evening (a rare treat for me) and came face to face with the reality we live in today. While the sun and my children were still up and shining bright, a burger commercial came on that featured a woman dressed in skin tight jeans and a revealing cut up tank top, seductively riding a mechanical bull with a burger in her hand. What?!! I remember thinking, "It's not even prime time yet." About that same time, this same fast food burger chain featured another rather inappropriate commercial of an American heiress dressed in a scanty swimsuit, seductively washing a car … and herself. And oh yeah, there was a glimpse of the burger in the commercial, too. To this one, I just sarcastically replied, "Wow … really?" Since when did we have to change the channel when commercials came on TV because our children were in the room?

Now, while these incidences may have been shocking to me, there are several generations behind me that are growing up thinking this kind of exposure is normal, to which we credit a nationwide—if not worldwide—numbness to sexual immorality. This generation coming up now is being conditioned to use their bodies and sex to gain attention and acceptance instead of using their talents and wit. They may argue that they, in fact, are using both, but what they don't understand is that the attraction to sex heavily overpowers the attraction to talent, because we are living in a sexually charged world. Your skills and talents hold a dim light to growing sexual interest.

These days, anything goes, but nobody is paying attention to the significant price people are paying for the freedom of sexual expression. Movies show people having casual premarital sex for the fun of it, with little or no sacrifice, and then moving on with their lives. This is not reality. In reality, people have casual premarital sex not *just* for fun and relief, but to temporarily boost their self esteem; going from partner to partner, looking for the next high or "true love," not ever really being fulfilled. In real life, when people have premarital sex—casual or committed—there are consequences like unplanned pregnancies (a compound problem), abortion, diseases, heartache, jealousy, worry, low self-esteem, anxieties, abandonment, disrespect, distrust, resentment, and even death. In real life when you have sex, it makes you deaf, dumb and blind to things you would never tolerate if you were sexually sober, creating shame, secrets, and the "I don't know why I do x-y-z" syndrome. Sure sex can be fun temporarily, but the side effects are always long term.

Now, you may disagree with me, even though you may have experiences with one or more of the negative side effects. You may even feel you are the exception because you have a good head on your shoulders and are very careful. But when it comes to premarital sex on your way to the altar, the rules change significantly, because you can't walk away from the consequences. You get to stick around to see every little negative side effect manifest and grow inside your marriage, built into its foundation. It would be difficult to list all the possible scenarios, but you may start to notice problems popping up in your marriage rooted in one of the side effects aforementioned. It may be directly related to your sex life or it may bleed into other areas. It may simply be that your sex life, that was once so exciting and amazing before you were married, may suddenly become comatose after you say, "I do." This is a crafty reversal trick of the enemy to get you on both sides: you cave in to your desires before you're married, then lose the desire after you're married. In actuality, you'd best serve yourself *and* your marriage by abating the desires before, then enjoying a lush harvest afterwards. Regardless of where you stand on this issue, sexual intimacy is a critically significant part of a healthy marriage, and its misuse or ignorance on how to approach it can cause crippling problems in a marriage quicker than you can finish sending out your wedding "thank you" notes—literally!

Word of Encouragement

Soon after I committed myself to a life of celibacy, I spoke to a friend of mine who had just gotten married, but had also lived a celibate life several years before meeting her husband. She shared with me that she had no idea how amazing sex could be until she got together with her husband after the wedding—and he was a virgin! She adamantly encouraged me to stay committed because God really does make good on this promise, in a big way. Part of me was like, "I don't know, I've had some pretty amazing sex …" But the other side of me was so curious, I had to know what she was talking about. Today, I can say with all confidence, it doesn't get better than this! But then again, that makes sense. What could possibly be better than *God's* best?

Just Me, Myself & I

If you are not sexually intimate with anyone … but yourself, you are **not** in the clear. Sex is for married people, because it creates an emotional and spiritual bond that is nearly indestructible. One of its benefits is the ability to keep two people together through the most difficult of times. Spiritually speaking, if you are engaging in masturbation, in most cases you are engaging in an act that requires your mind to go to a place that is just as damaging as having a person there with you. In Matthew 5:28 it says that if you even look at a person lustfully, you have committed adultery in your heart. Is it a sin to masturbate? No. There is no direct or indirect scripture to support this claim. However, what takes place in your mind before, during and after you masturbate is another issue. Since the Bible tells us that we should learn to control our bodies in a holy and honorable way and that all things are lawful, though they may not be beneficial, it's better to err on the side of safety and not engage in masturbation[35].

> *Frustration, disappointment, and alienation have no place in the bedroom.*

Physically and emotionally speaking, masturbation may create some obstacles in your married sex life. Sex is intended to be a selfless act between a husband and wife that focuses on bringing pleasure to each other. It is not "making love" as much as it is an "act of love." Masturbation is a self-centered act that focuses on your own gratification, and you may carry this thinking over into your marriage. If you have come into the habit of pleasing yourself, you now

---

[35] 1 Thessalonians 4:4-5; 1 Corinthians 6:12

have a very hard habit to break since you will—no doubt—prefer your own expertise to your husband's learning curve. Such obstacles can create frustration for both of you, and alienation toward him as you experience disappointment with his performance. This is an area in which your husband must feel needed and victorious. If you take that away from him, you have just welcomed in a brand new range of problems including—but not limited to—him seeking out someone who can actually appreciate him sexually. Frustration, disappointment, and alienation have no place in the bedroom.

Use Your Support

If you are ready to make a commitment to total celibacy, YOU WILL NEED SUPPORT. This is not the kind of thing you want to try to tackle alone. I remember times when I called up my close girl friend in times of weakness, pitifully trying to convince her how if I just called him "just to see how he was doing" it could do no harm. She could see right through my scheme and made me confront my true intentions. Whenever I did something that was questionable or appeared to be questionable, she called me on it. Confide in another godly woman or two whom you trust and who respect the decision you have made. Ask them if they would be available to you to hold you accountable for your actions, day and night. This means, when you know all you have to do is pick up the phone and Mr. Too Sexy for His Shirt will be at your place in no time, or when it's just you and your lovely right hand, you need to do two things: 1) call your girl who will talk you through it and remind you of the reason you made the commitment in the first place, and 2) immediately get on your feet and **DO SOMETHING ELSE;** run the stairs, jump-n-jacks, dance, go for a walk, leave the house, cook an elaborate meal, go for ice cream (my personal favorite)—anything that will physically take your mind off the act until the urges pass. I remember being home alone once and the feeling hit me like a tsunami. I only entertained the idea of relieving the tension for a few moments before I jumped up, grabbed my keys and went out the door. I didn't know where I was going, but I wasn't going down the road of setbacks and regrets.

One last piece of advice on how to be an overcomer in this situation: play defense. You know you. If you know that listening to certain kinds of music turn you on, avoid them. If you feel just a little too much like "hot stuff" when you wear your satin pajamas, save them for your husband. Don't set yourself up for failure. Avoid movies with heavy sexual overtones or ones that stir up your sexual passions. If you still associate with one of the men from Chapter 2, and the mere sight of him makes your heart flutter, stay away from him. And those dirty little "romance" novels that have you so intrigued, let them be. They encourage you to go places in your mind that only leads you to wonder, "What would it be like to …" Be smart. This challenge is not about how much you can get away *with* and stay celibate, but rather how much you can get away *from* and still be strong, attractive, and exciting.

Action for Chapter 7

"Flee sexual immorality. Every sin that a man does is outside the body, but he who commits sexual immorality sins against his own body. Or do you not know that your body is the temple of the Holy Spirit who is in you, whom you have from God, and you are not your own?" – I Corinthians 6:18-19

This action step is as intense and as important as "Personal Maintenance." With diligence, the rewards are indescribable and continuously offer more all the time.

Make a commitment and proclaim your new victory. Let it be known what you intend to accomplish. You'll need the support.

Clean house. Get rid of all sexual paraphernalia and protection. As long as you're protected and have the tools to make it more interesting, you're likely to engage in the act.

Keep a calendar and take it one day at a time. If you have a "mess up," just make a note of it and keep going. Just don't give up.

If applicable, contact your sexual partner(s) and let them know of your decision. Distance yourself from them. Change your phone number if you have to, and if he shows up at your door, don't open it. This is serious business. As long as there's a door between the two of you, he can't use his charm to make you weak.

Conclusion

Congratulations on completing the first stage in preparing for marriage. Your faithfulness and dedication will not go unrewarded. Take a couple of weeks off to review what you've learned, and re-implement any action steps that have fallen by the wayside. While this book is not an all-inclusive "get ready" guide, it does provide an excellent foundation on which to build your future marriage. Supplement the lessons here with the materials from the list of recommended reading and resources in Appendix 1, and you should be well on your way.

While each chapter gives an overview of the lessons, if a particular chapter really hits home for you, I encourage you to expand on that teaching and fully develop each principle in this book. There are so many resources available it can be difficult to choose one. If you don't know where to start, you can email me at the address below and I can point you in the right direction. Once you feel like you've gotten a good hold of the action steps in this book, you are ready to advance to Book 2: *Purposeful Courtship*, A No-Frills Guide to Selecting Your Soul Mate. This book will teach you what to focus on to get the most for your time while courting.

I'd love to hear how God has touched your life as a result of this work, what you've learned about yourself, and any testimonies that were created on your journey.

Please email me at:
info@mymarriageplans.com

Or send a letter to:
13337 South Street, Suite 136
Cerritos, CA 90703

Appendix 1: References

How to Enter into a Relationship with Christ

If you have never received Jesus Christ into your heart and have a genuine interest in beginning your relationship with Him, all you have to do is recite aloud the prayer below with sincerity:

> God I know that I need you in my life. Please forgive me for my past sins and heal the brokenness in my life. Jesus, I believe in my heart that you died on the cross and were raised from the dead for my sins. Come into my heart and live in me. Send your Holy Spirit to help me do your will for the rest of my days. Thank you for giving me the opportunity to know you better.
> In Jesus' name, Amen.

If you said that prayer with sincerity, you are now saved. Welcome to God's Kingdom! In order for you to really see God's hand move in your life, it is imperative that you get connected with a church home and someone mature in God's Word who will begin to disciple you in your new walk. God has great things in store for you!

Recommended Reading

- *Fasting*, Jentezen Franklin
- *The Power of Purpose & Vision*, Dr. Myles Munroe
- *Captivating*, John & Stasi Eldredge
- *Knight in Shining Armor*, P.B. Wilson
- *Understanding the Purpose & Power of Men*, Dr. Myles Munroe
- *Understanding the Purpose & Power of Woman*, Dr. Myles Munroe
- *The Dream Giver*, Bruce Wilkinson
- *How People Grow*, Dr. Henry Cloud & Dr. John Townsend

Recommended Resources

One of the best things you can do for your new or future marriage is become a better you.

- Klemmer & Associates – the premier leadership and character development company. For life changing seminars and resources call (800) 577-5447 or visit their website www.klemmer.com
- Summit Institute – Experience authentic transformation, discover your God given destiny and become all that God has called you to be. Located in West Covina, California, as part of Faith Community Church, you can visit their website www.go2faith.com/education/summit_institute/ or call (626) 858-8400 x1597

Upcoming Books

In the prenuptial series:

- Book 2: *Purposeful Courtship*, A No-Frills Guide to Selecting Your Soul Mate
- Book 3: *Engaging Yourself*, How Your Engagement is So Much More Than Wedding Planning

Post-nuptial

- *After the Ceremony*, How to Get Your Marriage Off to a Running Start Without All the Usual Obstacles

More from Marriage PLANS

Get all that Marriage PLANS has to offer and make an investment in the health, longevity, and joy of your new or future marriage.

- Small Group Studies – Experience *Before He Finds You* hands on. Be challenged in your journey to becoming a virtuous wife and a better you. Have your questions answered, develop lasting

Appendix 1: References

relationships and learn from other women as you take on this intense 8-week study.

- Weekend Seminar – Get a complete overview of the prenuptial series: Books 1, 2 and 3 in a fast-paced, life-changing weekend.
- One-day Seminar – How can just a couple of hours impact your entire future? Spend it in this one-day seminar on, "The Ten Best Things You Can Do For Your Marriage *Before* You Get Married." This seminar highlights the top ten critical points from the prenuptial series to put you on the path to marital wisdom and success.

For more information, write to: info@mymarriageplans.com

Appendix 2: Questionnaire

Chapter 6 Purpose Questionnaire

This questionnaire is printed with the permission of Joe Martin, RealworldUniversity.com. "RealWorld University's (RWU) mission is to help students succeed in college and in life by helping them identify and pursue their purpose, strengthen their character, overcome life's obstacles, and maximize their potential. RWU addresses some of the toughest challenges facing college students today by sharing proven strategies, solutions, and advice from some of the country's leading educators, authors, speakers, and college graduates."

Your purpose is not something you create; it was already created for you. I call this the "promise." Our job is to uncover our unique talents, skills, and abilities (i.e., our gifts) and use them to serve others for the purpose of our Creator. Therefore, our purpose is the same; the only difference is the vehicle in which we choose to pursue it.

Listed below are some strategies that will help you uncover your uniqueness. How you choose to use those gifts to serve others will be entirely up to you.

	Please start by doing the following:
1	Eliminate all distractions (no phone, television, music, etc.). Find a quiet place.
2	Imagine you just woke up from a coma, and you don't remember your friends, enemies, family, society norms and/or expectations (you only remember what you're good at and what you love to do).

3	Pretend you only have one year to live (in perfect health), and your bills and other financial responsibilities are of no concern to you.
4	Pray to God that He will reveal your purpose through these questions.
5	Suspend all judgment as you answer each question listed below (i.e., answer with your heart, not with your head -- that's how God speaks to us).
6	Be totally honest with yourself as you answer each question. Set aside some time (however long it takes) to write down your responses (don't erase).

Investigative Questions: Who are you?	
1	If you had the time, what would you most want to study, practice, master, or research deeply? What would you want to be an expert in?
2	What activities do you engage in or talk about, and you lose track of all sense of time?

Appendix 2: Questionnaire

3	Through what particular skill(s) or ability(ies) have you received the most compliments?
4	If money wasn't a concern, what work would you be willing to do for FREE?
5	What personal talents, skills, and abilities do YOU have the most confidence in?
6	What ONE thing would you dare to attempt if you could not fail?
7	If you only had six months to live (in perfect health), other than family and spiritual activities, what activities or tasks would you engage in?
8	Describe the "*perfect JOB*" (not life) in terms of duties, activities, and responsibilities.

9	What professional activities give you the greatest pleasure, make you the happiest, give you the most fulfillment, greatest peace of mind, and the most satisfaction?
10	From your previous responses, what activities/skills tend to be repeating themselves (*list them here and use them while answering questions 11 - 15*)?

	Commitment Questions: How committed are you?
11	Are you willing to dedicate your life to this? (i.e., is the reward worth the risk?)
12	Are you willing to pay the price for it (i.e., sacrifice, face your fears, break bad habits, make necessary changes, make tough decisions, handle the setbacks, etc.)?
13	Have you ever envisioned yourself doing this (i.e., can you FEEL it, SEE it and DESCRIBE it in great detail, and even almost TOUCH it)?

Appendix 2: Questionnaire

14	If you won the lotto tomorrow, would you still pursue it?
15	Is this something you FEEL you MUST do? Does it FEEL right?

If you are still unsure about your "calling," proceed to questions 16 - 28.

If you are pretty certain about your calling at this point, proceed to questions 29 - 33.

Still uncertain? See if these questions can help. Again, write down your responses.

	Additional Investigative Questions: Who are you?
16	If God were to tell you right now that it would be possible for you to accomplish one great thing while you're here on earth, what would you want it to be?
17	What five wonderful things could God do with you, for you, through you, in you, for the rest of your life?

18	What are you confident in doing now that you knew nothing about a few years ago?
19	What are the greatest opportunities for you in each of the following areas: 1.) your family; 2.) your job; 3.) your church; 4.) your community?
20	What crazy ideas about your future have you dismissed recently? Why?
21	What talents and/or abilities seem to naturally flow out of you?
22	In what areas do you normally produce good results?

Appendix 2: Questionnaire

	Passion Questions: What gets your juices flowing?
23	What do you think about when you lie awake at night just staring at the ceiling?
24	What kind of issues, needs, opportunities, activities, and ideas really motivate you and seem to give you energy?
25	What things/issues deeply concern you?
26	What dreams or visions are almost impossible to put out of your head?
27	To what can you give 100% of yourself for your whole life?

28	From your previous responses, what activities, skills, and/or ideas, tend to be repeating themselves (list them now and use them while answering questions 11 - 15 on the previous page)?

Integrity Questions: Whom are you "really" serving?

Your purpose is only as pure as your motives. Your gifts can either be used positively or negatively. Before you begin your journey in pursuit of purpose, you should honestly ask and answer the following questions (write it down):

29	**Why** do I really want to do this?
30	Am I doing this for my own selfish desires?
31	Will I be able to put God first in my life if I pursue this?

Appendix 2: Questionnaire

32	Would I be able to use my gifts and talents if I pursued this?
33	Would this bring out the best in me?

"The purpose of life is to have a life with a purpose." -- Robert Byrne

Believe it or not, this is only the beginning. Pursuing your purpose is a life-long process (but an exciting and very fulfilling one). After you have identified your talents, abilities, and skills (i.e., gifts), you must ask yourself: How can I use these gifts to serve others while serving my Creator?

For more information regarding this questionnaire or RealWorld University, go to:

http://www.rwuniversity.com/

Appendix 3: Calendar

18-Month Fill-in Calendar – Document important dates in your journey and keep track of your appointments and dates with the One worthy of your affections.

Month: ______________________________ Year: ____________

Sun	Mon	Tue	Wed	Thu	Fri	Sat

Month: ______________________ Year: __________

Sun	Mon	Tue	Wed	Thu	Fri	Sat

Calendar

Month: ______________________________ Year: ____________

Sun	Mon	Tue	Wed	Thu	Fri	Sat

Month: ____________________ Year: __________

Sun	Mon	Tue	Wed	Thu	Fri	Sat

Calendar

Month: ______________________________ Year: ____________

Sun	Mon	Tue	Wed	Thu	Fri	Sat

Month: ______________________________ Year: ____________

Sun	Mon	Tue	Wed	Thu	Fri	Sat

Calendar

Month: ______________________ Year: __________

Sun	Mon	Tue	Wed	Thu	Fri	Sat

Month: ______________________________ Year: ____________

Sun	Mon	Tue	Wed	Thu	Fri	Sat

Calendar

Month: ______________________________ Year: ____________

Sun	Mon	Tue	Wed	Thu	Fri	Sat

Month: ______________________________ Year: ____________

Sun	Mon	Tue	Wed	Thu	Fri	Sat

Calendar

Month: ______________________ Year: __________

Sun	Mon	Tue	Wed	Thu	Fri	Sat

Month: ______________________________ Year: ____________

Sun	Mon	Tue	Wed	Thu	Fri	Sat

Calendar

Month: ______________________________ Year: ____________

Sun	Mon	Tue	Wed	Thu	Fri	Sat

Month: ______________________________ Year: ____________

Sun	Mon	Tue	Wed	Thu	Fri	Sat

Calendar

Month: ______________________________ Year: ____________

Sun	Mon	Tue	Wed	Thu	Fri	Sat

Month: ______________________________ Year: ____________

Sun	Mon	Tue	Wed	Thu	Fri	Sat

Calendar

Month: ______________________________ Year: ____________

Sun	Mon	Tue	Wed	Thu	Fri	Sat

Month: ______________________________ Year: ____________

Sun	Mon	Tue	Wed	Thu	Fri	Sat

Appendix 4: Journal

Journal – Keeping a written record of your ups and downs, trials and triumphs make for an excellent testimony to share with others and strengthens your faith in our God who never fails us. It is one of the best ways to see God working in your life.

Journal

Journal

Journal

Journal

Journal

Journal

Journal

Journal

Journal

Journal

Journal

Journal

Journal

Journal

Journal

Journal

Journal

Journal

Journal

Journal

Journal

Journal

Journal

Journal